CONNECTED **C**OMMUNI
Creating a new knowledge land

RE-IMAGINING CONTESTED COMMUNITIES

Connecting Rotherham through research

Edited by Elizabeth Campbell, Kate Pahl,
Elizabeth Pente and Zanib Rasool

First published in Great Britain in 2018 by

Policy Press
University of Bristol
1-9 Old Park Hill
Bristol
BS2 8BB
UK
t: +44 (0)117 954 5940
pp-info@bristol.ac.uk
www.policypress.co.uk

North America office:
Policy Press
c/o The University of Chicago Press
1427 East 60th Street
Chicago, IL 60637, USA
t: +1 773 702 7700
f: +1 773-702-9756
sales@press.uchicago.edu
www.press.uchicago.edu

British Library Cataloguing in Publication Data
A catalogue record for this book is available from the British Library

Library of Congress Cataloging-in-Publication Data
A catalog record for this book has been requested

ISBN 978-1-4473-3332-6 paperback
ISBN 978-1-4473-3330-2 hardcover
ISBN 978-1-4473-3333-3 ePub
ISBN 978-1-4473-3334-0 Mobi
ISBN 978-1-4473-3331-9 ePdf

Cover design by Hayes Design
Front cover image: istock
Printed and bound in Great Britain by CMP, Poole
Policy Press uses environmentally responsible print partners

Contents

List of figures

Chapter Twenty-one

Notes on contributors

Ryan Bramley is a PhD candidate in the School of Education, University of Sheffield. He is writing a thesis on 'Filmmaking as a community building practice'. He completed a master's degree in August 2016, culminating in a dissertation project, 'Non-professional poetic representations of the 1984-85 Miners' Strike in industrial/ post-industrial South Yorkshire' – a socio-literary comparative study of the poetry catalysed by the Miners' Strike, both during that conflict and from the present day.

Deborah Bullivant is an educationalist with over 30 years' experience from working across ages, within communities. She is the director of 'Grimm and Co' a not-for-profit literacy charity, based in Rotherham. The group of girls involved in the 'We come from' programme are classed by the wider community as 'Roma'. However, they don't recognise this term and would prefer to describe themselves as being born in their country of origin (in this case, Czech Republic, Hungary and Slovakia) but now citizens of the UK. These girls are aged between 11 and 15 and were co-researchers within this study – focusing on autobiographical journeys during times of turmoil and uncertainty for their community in Rotherham.

Elizabeth (Beth) Campbell's interests are in collaborative and community-based research and writing. Her current research explores the constitutive nature of collaborative research, and especially how it works – through shared agency, commitment and experience – to form and transform those who engage it. She is co-author of *Doing ethnography today* and *The other side of Middletown*, and is Associate Professor in Marshall University's College of Education in the US, where she teaches qualitative research and educational foundations.

Miles Crompton is a Policy and Partnership Officer at Rotherham Metropolitan Borough Council (MBC) with a remit for research and policy development. Miles graduated with a degree in town planning in 1984 and worked in town planning for 15 years, before moving to corporate research, while working for Barnsley MBC (1989-2005). He became Research Co-ordinator at Rotherham MBC in 2005 and has worked at Rotherham Council ever since. He also served as a councillor in Leeds from 1987 to 1995 and has been a director of South Yorkshire Credit Union since 2002. With 30 years' experience in local government, Miles has taken a keen interest in demographic and socioeconomic trends affecting South Yorkshire, and in developing a better understanding of local communities.

Tanya Evans is a mother of two girls, and has lived in Rotherham all her life. She has been actively involved in her local community, local children's centre and community research for a number of years.

Nathan Gibson is a photographer and filmmaker, whose work focuses on community cohesion, contemporary masculinity and companionship. During the spring and summer of 2016, Nathan worked with a group of young men in Rotherham to create a collaborative photographic project detailing and discussing their experiences of living in the town. Nathan recently moved to Beijing, where he is pursuing a master's degree in multimedia journalism.

William Gould's current research concerns notions of citizenship and state transformation over Indian independence and partition. He is also continuing to research and write on the politics of religious conflict and 'communalism' in South Asia, for which he is currently working on a third book project 'Religion and conflict in South Asia'. He is also working on historical narratives of South Asian migrants to the UK after 1947, as part of a collaborative project with other members of the University of Leeds.

Abi Hackett is a mother of two and a Research Fellow at Manchester Metropolitan University. Her ethnographic research mainly focuses on the meaning making of very young children, and how to understand these collaboratively with parents and families. Before completing her doctorate, Abi worked in the cultural sector, specialising in learning and community engagement, for a number of years, including as Community Outreach Officer at Clifton Park Museum. She is co-editor of the book *Children's spatialities. Embodiment, emotion, agency.*

Ray Hearne is a writer and performer of songs and poems. He worked for many years with schools and community groups across South Yorkshire and beyond, to find their own poems, performance pieces, songs and anthems. He was Musical Director of Rotherham's 2011 Hearts of Steel project and a contributing writer to BBC Radio 2's 'Radio Ballads' series. In 2013, Ray's poem 'A sing song for stainless steel' was cut into 14 benches now sited along the Moor in Sheffield

City centre. Ray is Chair of Grimm and Co in Rotherham, and Chair of No Masters Co-operative.

Marcus Hurcombe is a youth worker with some 20 years' experience in the local authority. He is a specialist in supporting marginalised boys and young men. His research interests include objects and hidden connectivity, young people and hidden literacy. He is now Principal of Lapis Philosophorum, a youth work consultancy and think tank.

Luke Eric Lassiter is Professor of Humanities and Anthropology, Director of Marshall University's Graduate Humanities Program in the US, and a recipient of the Margaret Mead Award. Eric is an internationally known anthropologist, who has published widely on ethnographic and collaborative research. His works include: *The Chicago guide to collaborative ethnography* and *Invitation to anthropology* (author); *The other side of Middletown* and *Doing ethnography today* (co-author); and *Collaborative anthropologies* (founding editor).

Cassie Limb is a process-based multi-media creative artist, working to provide immersive experiences for the individual, and which emotionally connect us with ourselves as well as with others in positive developmental outcomes.

Khalida Luqman is a community activist working in the Rotherham community for over 30 years. Khalida specialises in mental health, working with hard-to-reach, non-literate, isolated women, to support them with their cultural and identity issues in order to widen their knowledge and education.

Joanna Magagula is a mother of two. For Joanna, this was an introductory experience into collaborative research. Joanna has a keen interest in the welfare and development of children and has volunteered at children's centres.

Maria O'Beirne is a senior analyst in the Department for Communities and Local Government (DCLG), providing support for policy areas on integration, faith and equalities. Maria has worked as a social researcher in government for over 13 years, working at the Home Office, the Health and Safety Executive, the Department for Work and Pensions and, more recently, in the DCLG. Prior to joining the Civil Service, Maria worked in Royal Holloway University of London as a researcher on the ESRC-funded Violence Research Programme, where she completed her PhD in sociology. Maria's early career was as a freelance researcher in Ireland, working for government and third sector organisations on social policy issues.

Kate Pahl is Professor of Arts and Literacy at Manchester Metropolitan University. She is the principle Investigator of the 'Imagine' project. She has worked in Rotherham for many years, first on the 'Every Object tells a Story' project with Zahir Rafiq and then with Deborah Bullivant on the 'Inspire Rotherham' project in 2009-11. She is the author of *Materializing Literacies in Communities* (London: Bloomsbury) and teaches on the doctoral programmes at the University of Sheffield.

Elizabeth Pente is a doctoral student at the University of Huddersfield. Her research is concerned with public history and post-Second World War urban decline and regeneration in the United Kingdom, with a focus on the co-production of historical knowledge. She received a BSc in Archaeology and Geology from Dickinson College in 2007 and an MA in Historical Studies with a concentration in Public History from the University of Maryland, Baltimore County in 2013. She is co-editor of *Re-imagining contested communities*, as part of the *'Imagine': Connecting Communities Through Research* project, funded by the ESRC.

Steve Pool originally trained as a sculptor. He now works as a visual artist in multiple medias to help people realise ideas, often making physical objects or changing environments. For the past 30 years, he has worked on many programmes and initiatives, including Creative Partnerships, public understanding of science and regeneration to area-based renewal programmes. Central to his work is the belief that access to new technologies offers many opportunities for people to produce – as well as to consume – culture.

Zahir Rafiq is an artist from Rotherham, South Yorkshire. He specialises in contemporary Islamic art, where he fuses traditional Islam motifs with western artistic styles. With this approach he sought to express not only a new way of looking at Islamic art, but also his own identity as someone being brought up as a Muslim in Britain.

Zanib Rasool, MBE, has worked in the voluntary and community sector for 30 years. Her work has been around the capacity building and voice of women and young people, and developing community cohesion projects and partnership work.

Robert Rutherfoord is a Principal Research Officer in the Department for Communities and Local Government with a background in social anthropology and development studies. He is responsible for analysis on decentralisation to neighbourhoods and community cohesion. He has a particular interest in linking up the Civil Service with academic research, to help share insights and solve problems. Previous roles included research on regeneration, neighbourhood planning, spatial analysis, and small business.

Mariam Shah was born and brought up in Rotherham. Her roles included community activism, youth and inter-faith work. She is mum to four children and the first female Muslim Chaplain in Rotherham. Her previous roles include Chair of Apna Haq and Muslim Rep for Standing Advisory Council for Religious Education (SACRE). She is also a trustee with 'Who Is Your Neighbour' since 2009. She is currently working with a number of organisations to develop a toolkit to help raise awareness of child sexual exploitation for parents, carers and vulnerable young people.

Shahin Shah trained at Rotherham College of Arts and Technology and the University Centre in Barnsley. She is known for her henna decorations and colourful artwork. She has worked for the 'Imagine' project as an artist, bringing her own unique vision to the themes of 'Imagine'.

Paul Ward is Professor of Modern British History at the University of Huddersfield and researches national identities in the UK in the 19th and 20th centuries. Recently he has been considering the co-production of historical knowledge and how communities think about their histories. He is author of four books, including *Britishness since 1870* (2004) and *Huw T. Edwards: British Labour and Welsh Socialism* (2011). He is currently co-writing and co-editing a book called *Co-producing research: A community development approach*, as part of the *'Imagine': Connecting Communities Through Research* project funded by the ESRC.

Acknowledgements

We would like to thank the following, who have helped in the preparation and writing of this book:

- the 'Imagine' team, including: Graham Crow, Sarah Banks, Angie Hart, Paul Ward and Angela Warren; special thanks to Graham, whose imagination and hard work brought us all together in the first place;
- the Economic and Social Research Council (ESRC), who funded the 'Imagine' project, grant number ES/K002686/2, and in particular, Christina Rowley and Lyndy Griffin;
- the Arts and Humanities Research Council (AHRC), with special thanks to Keri Facer and Gary Grubb;
- the Department for Communities and Local Government, in particular Robert Rutherfoord;
- Deborah Bullivant would like to say thank you to: Eirian Burke, Jennifer Booth, Sophie Turner, and Laura Jenova and the Clifton University Girls;
- community organisations in Rotherham, especially:
  - Al-muneera
  - Clifton Park Museum
  - Clifton Partnership
  - Coleridge Children's Centre
  - Grimm and Company
  - Mowbray Gardens Library
  - Rotherham Cultural Services
  - Rotherham Ethnic Minority Alliance (REMA)
  - Rotherham Libraries
  - Rotherham Metropolitan Borough Council
  - Rotherham United Community Sports Trust
  - Rotherham Youth Services
  - Tassibee
  - Thornhill School

Acknowledgements

The following people in particular have supported our work and we would like to say thank you to:

- Zaidah Ahmed
- Debjani Chatterjee
- Alnaar Clayton
- Alison Gilchrist
- Libby Hicken
- Susan Hyatt
- Christl Kettle
- Helen Mort
- Irna Qureshi
- Shirin Teifouri

Series editors' foreword

Around the globe, communities of all shapes and sizes are increasingly seeking an active role in producing knowledge about how to understand, represent and shape their world for the better. At the same time, academic research is increasingly realising the critical importance of community knowledge in producing robust insights into contemporary change in all fields. New collaborations, networks, relationships and dialogues are being formed between academic and community partners, characterised by a radical intermingling of disciplinary traditions and by creative methodological experimentation.

There is a groundswell of research practice that aims to build new knowledge, address longstanding silences and exclusions, and pluralise the forms of knowledge used to inform common sense understandings of the world.

The aim of this book series is to act as a magnet and focus for the research that emerges from this work. Originating from the UK Arts and Humanities Research Council's Connected Communities programme (www.connected-communities.org), the series showcases critical discussion of the latest methods and theoretical resources for combining academic and public knowledge via high-quality, creative, engaged research. It connects the emergent practice happening around the world with the longstanding and highly diverse traditions of engaged and collaborative practice from which that practice draws.

This series seeks to engage a wide audience of academic and community researchers, policy makers and others with an interest in how to combine academic and public expertise. The wide range of publications in the series demonstrate that this field of work is helping to reshape the knowledge landscape as a site of democratic dialogue and collaborative practice, as well as contestation and imagination. The series editors welcome approaches from academic and community researchers working in this field who have a distinctive contribution to make to these debates and practices today.

Keri Facer, Professor of Educational and Social Futures,
University of Bristol

George McKay, Professor of Media Studies,
University of East Anglia

Part One
Introductions

ONE

What kind of book is this?

Elizabeth Campbell

Readers expect texts to follow particular forms. Readers of novels expect fleshed-out characters, who struggle with each other and with events. Newspaper readers expect the same sections, in the same order, every day. Those who read assembly manuals expect to be guided – ideally, with some degree of clarity – through the assembly process.

Readers of community-based and academic texts have expectations, too. Community texts often celebrate local personalities and events in ways that say something important about local experiences, identities and values. Academic texts usually make evidence-based original claims and arguments, in ways that say something about the author's intelligence, training and rigour. Both kinds of texts are aimed at very specific audiences, which have different priorities and expectations and are likely to struggle in finding value in the other's traditions of knowledge production. Academic readers may find community texts not critical or thorough enough; community readers may find academic texts neither accessible nor relevant.

This book is an experimental text, aimed at both academic and community readers; thus, it both enacts and disrupts the expectations of both audiences. It is produced by people situated at various points within and across universities and communities, who believe that knowledge production is not limited to particular kinds of writers and audiences. Moreover, the artists, academics, students, parents, community development workers and community members whose words (and images) you will find in these pages have intentionally breached these boundaries, because we find real value in the knowledge we can produce together.

In some ways, this book is like a collection of essays. Essay collections bring together pieces that may or may not reference each other, build on each other or flow together, although they all address the same central topic. But this is also more than a collection of essays. Although its central topic is the South Yorkshire community of Rotherham, the collaboration that produced this book is as much a part of this text as the community that stands at its centre. Over the course of three years, a group of people, who initially came together to plan the research for the 'Imagine' project,[1] collaborated on research, exhibitions, actions and, most recently, this book. Although the forms, languages and discourses we use differ, we all value what each of us has to say.

Academics who want to better understand this book might look to developments such as experimental ethnography and community literacy. This book is a little like the experimental texts that began to emerge in ethnographic and related literatures in the 1960s and 1970s, and burst onto the scene in the 1980s, during what came to be called 'the experimental moment in the human sciences' (Marcus and Fischer, 1986). A defining characteristic of experimental ethnography was – and remains – a willingness to be open, and to experiment with textual production and forms. Some of the earliest experimental ethnographies focused on dialogue, and on issues of voice and representation. Today's experimentalists and their interlocutors continue to wrestle with questions such as 'What counts for knowledge?' and 'Who speaks for whom?'.

This text also fits within the very broad range of disruptive, multi-vocal and hybrid texts that have emerged out of community literacy, which Peck et al (1994) described as a:

> type of discourse that, like cultural critique, seeks to acknowledge difference rather than absorb it ... [C]ommunity literacy envisions a rhetoric of inquiry, where multiple positions and perspectives are considered to reach mutual goals. In place of multicultural programs of simply appreciating or becoming consumers of difference and diversity, this discourse works toward an intercultural conversation for the purpose of change. (Peck et al, 1994, p.15)

An 'intercultural conversation' may be the best way to think about this book. Its collaborators hail from different histories, universities, ethnicities, professions, disciplines, neighbourhoods, classes, religions and context. Although all share an experience of Rotherham, those experiences are very particular, and can be both similar and different. Throughout the time we have worked together, we have maintained a commitment not just to ourselves and to the project, but also to recognising and working across our differences. That commitment, we hope, is present in this text as well, which embraces a very particular difference that has long been at the heart of the Rotherham project: that of voice. The heteroglossia at the core of this collaboration is allowed to speak for itself in this book; we have explicitly chosen not to smooth all the many voices into one, nor have we sought to normalise the text. As a narrative strategy it may be unfamiliar – even disconcerting – to some readers, but we think it provides an authentic view into this particular intercultural conversation. If an image will help, imagine that you have just opened the doors of a community centre, and stepped into a loud, lively and diverse meeting of people from different perspectives and walks of life, all of whom are sharing with each other their experiences of this community.

We want to emphasise that although the work in these pages takes up an actual and important conversation about a place called Rotherham, it is not meant to stand in for all conversations about Rotherham, much less for all places that share similarities or histories. Our goal is to invite you into a conversation about this community, and to think about how knowledge is produced in the many communities we are all part of. We are committed to the idea that communities produce their own forms of knowledge, and that those forms are valid – and valuable – ways of knowing. We hope that once you have read and considered what is here, you will agree.

We want to articulate the value of this kind of research for community knowledge production that is emergent, situated and future oriented, and we would like to invite you, as readers, to engage with us as co-inquirers. Some of you may be students interested in collaborative projects. When you read our sections on collaboration, you might like to ask yourself the following questions:

- Whose voices count in collaborations and why?
- What do you do when you don't agree?
- How can universities make things better in some way?

We also would like people reading this who are researchers to think about whether this book has made them think differently about ways of researching communities. Questions here might include:

- What kinds of voices do artistic modes of enquiry let in?
- What are the limitations of linguistically oriented research methods?
- How does history contribute to an understanding of communities in the everyday?
- How do we incorporate diverse voices in research?

As they read this book, we would also like people to think about all the places where they have lived. Think about the different ways we, as humans, experience community, and consider the following questions:

- What are your earliest memories of the place where you grew up?
- How do places emerge in your mind – as smells, sights, voices or feelings?
- What kinds of experiences shape the way you understand place?
- Can places change and how do they change?

Our voices here are not definitive. They share some characteristics, in that they are hopeful, committed and unique to this book. We recognise our own partiality and we would want to engage with you, the reader, as someone who also might disagree with us, or who might not like what you read. But we would like you to recognise the nature of this research as emergent, not fixed and contingent on experience, identity and cultures. This is 'living knowledge' that is constructed together (see Facer and Enright, 2016). We do not 'know' all there is to know about Rotherham in this book, but we have worked together to produce a braided account of what we have known and experienced as co-researchers. We hope you enjoy our work. In these pages is knowledge that we have all shared with each other. Now, we would like to share this with you.

Note

1   These initial people were: Deborah Bullivant, Marcus Hurcombe, Khalida Luqman, Zahir Rafiq, Zanib Rasool, Mariam Shah and Shahin Shah. The original team were also pleased to be working with Paul Ward, Elizabeth Pente, Elizabeth Campbell and Eric Lassiter. Our advisory board included Miles Compton, from Rotherham Metropolitan Borough Council. Our project was linked to work that Abigail Hackett and Steve Pool were doing with parents in Rotherham. Steve Pool was also the artist in residence on the 'Imagine' project. Kate Pahl had also previously worked with William Gould and Ray Hearne and was working with Ryan Bramley, on the industrial heritage and histories of Rotherham. We were later joined by Cassie Limb, artist, and were also grateful for the support of the 'Imagine' team, as well as many other community organisations in Rotherham, listed in the acknowledgements.

TWO

Policy, practice and racism: social cohesion in action

Zanib Rasool

How does a community redefine itself after events that undermine social cohesion at neighbourhood, national and global level? How can communities influence neighbourhood policies and have a voice? These are questions that are central to policy development.

The concept of social cohesion in neighbourhoods is currently a key policy issue, with the context for this including internal conflicts between groups competing for the same scarce resources, structural inequality, housing and environment neglect, crime and disorder, creating segregation and a culture of 'us and them'. We, the research team, found that found that arts methodology was a tool for ethnic minority women and young people to negotiate boundaries and hostile territories and to engage in policy questions on community cohesion through photography, portraits and poetry (see Chapter Eighteen, Chapter Nineteen and Chapter Twenty-one in this book).

Hoggett (1997) argues that policies are often made in ignorance of the complexity within communities. This book is about communities in Rotherham, but it is also a book about 'every' northern British town in the grip of post-industrialisation and post-colonialism. The current way policies are developed and put into practice is not working for the people living in such communities. This book asks how alternative ways of knowing in neighbourhoods can inform government policy within contested or fractured communities. The answer, we believe, is in the methodology that this book advocates. This includes collaborative ethnography, co-production and arts practice. These methodologies are communicative and situated within the everyday and cultural contexts of communities.

Policy impacts on all areas of community life. This book engages with a number of policy areas, including:

- the work of early years settings and the importance of listening to parental views;

- community cohesion and diversity;
- working with socially excluded young people and providing them with a platform to have a voice.

Our book highlights the importance of the capacity building of women through writing groups and community-based projects that support women's activism and that give them the confidence to speak out. It is vitally important that all sectors of the community are central in policy making; often, the best people to drive policy are the communities who are experts on their own lives.

National policy makers often do not see the daily barriers that ordinary people face and their resilience and creativity to survive the everyday. Policy planning at arm's length often means that policies do not consider the reality of people's lives. When it comes to documenting and exploring the challenges that communities face, it is the members of the community who are best placed to provide solutions to issues such as crime and disorder, social housing and community cohesion.

Often, policy text can also be disparaging, and certain language can further stigmatise communities. Words such as 'disadvantaged' and 'deprived' get mentioned repeatedly in policies; but who defines 'disadvantaged'? Communities would not describe themselves in such terms. An overreliance on neighborhood statistics can lead to planning from a deficit model as people are grouped collectively and individuals' skills and knowledge are lost. Communities can develop their own strategies to address neighbourhood issues, youth nuisance or isolation of the elderly through small-scale projects, of which there are many examples across the country.

Sometimes, when people are repeatedly told what is good for them, it can lead to resistance. Too often, those in power take a broad-brush approach to policy development, and overlook the diversity within communities. This results in problematic assumptions being made about communities, and the policies enacted tend to fail. A policy cannot encompass everyone who happens to live in a particular neighbourhood or who is from a certain social group. The diversity within neighbourhoods needs to be acknowledged and, therefore, policies cannot be developed from a 'one size fits all' perspective. Certain communities have been defined as disadvantaged by policy makers for years. They have been marginalised and told they have no skills or capital to achieve anything without various state interventions. There seems to be a disconnect between policies, with overzealousness in dictating in the private sphere to parents and then giving control over the public sphere to the same members of the community.

In the past, policies tended to be paternalistic and focused on policy makers' perceptions of community needs. They often overlooked individual skills and knowledge within communities that could be utilised for the betterment of that community. This paternalistic approach disempowered communities and further pushed them to the margins. Members of the community were not encouraged to be involved in putting policies into action. McKinlay (2006) argues that: 'empowering communities requires councils to move from a regulatory/compliance control mode to a facilitative mode – a shift from "Council knows best" to "Community knows best"' (p.496). It is very hard for decision makers to shift some of the power and control to communities. Despite calls for this move, it has been slow to become a reality.

There have been recent shifts to decentralisation in the UK, with the Department for Communities and Local Government giving more control to local communities and citizens, supposedly allowing communities to do things differently with more accountability to local people. As a community worker, I know there has been a move in policy making to consult with communities. However, consultation can be an empty process and tokenistic, if people feel that their views are not being taken into account. An example in my community was a process of consulting women on the building of, and access to, new swimming facilities. During the consultation, women were asked about suitable times for them. However, the decision makers on timetabling swimming sessions ignored what the women had said, and opened women-only sessions at a time when many of the women would be doing the morning school run. This sort of tokenistic gesture leads to women not wanting to engage in future consultation.

Rather than the community initiating ideas on policy, it is often the case that government officials come to the community with questions that have already been formed to elicit a desired response. As McKinlay (2006) argues, often 'citizens are consulted on the Council's answers to the Council's own questions' (p.493). Additionally, participation techniques can be problematic, as policies tend to gravitate towards certain voices and to exclude others. Skidmore et al (2006) provide considerable evidence to 'show how participation can disempower communities by co-opting so called community leaders and leaving the actual communities behind' (p.6). Men tend to be elevated to community leader positions. They then represent the whole of their particular community and the voices of women and the young in policy are left out.

For effective consultation to occur, policy makers need to recognise that communities are made up of multiple voices. There needs to be equality of voice in developing policies. This requires genuine attempts to engage those in the community who are harder to reach and who do not often have a voice in policy development, such as ethnic minority women. Carby (1996) argues that Black women are subject to the simultaneous oppression of patriarchy, class and race that is different to White women's experiences, and those experiences are often invisible in policy. It is also disempowering if white women start representing the voice of minority women. To achieve meaningful consultation, policy writers need to talk directly to ordinary people – the exhausted mother, the lonely older person who feels forgotten, the disengaged young man. To talk to people, you need to go into those communities – the run-down council estate, the school, the pub or the street corners where you find young people kicking the ball about every night since their local youth centre has closed.

I believe that policy makers need to acknowledge that communities are where political, cultural and social knowledge is created every day and histories are made; communities also have the solution, if only local authorities worked with them in a less disempowering way as people should not be viewed as 'empty vessels': people have life experiences through which they gain knowledge and they are best placed to make change happen. This book calls for a serious reassessment of how policies are developed and written, and calls on policy makers to work towards engaging ordinary people in communities in a more equitable and meaningful way, to allow them to have a voice in the solutions to the social issues that they face.

Racism and the implications for community cohesion

In the current political climate, in the wake of Brexit, the election of Donald Trump and the rise of neo-nationalist and alt-right movements around the world, the issue of engaging communities more effectively in the development of policies is more important than ever. Policy makers and elites were too far removed from community life and were caught off guard by these developments. They did not foresee the discontent of their citizens and the political disengagement that resulted in these events. If we learn anything from both the shifting political tides and our failures to notice those shifts, it must be that big data alone cannot tell us all we need to know about community life. We need to be on the ground, working collaboratively with communities, if we are to develop meaningful and relevant policy.

As a nation, we in Great Britain pride ourselves on being a tolerant country that celebrates multiculturalism and diversity, a place where everyone is treated equally and with fairness. However, in recent years, racism has been on the rise, with events reminiscent of the 1970s. The current rise in Islamophobia globally towards Muslims like myself is unjustified. 'Prejudice and discrimination against Muslims has increased dramatically over the last decade. Muslims suffer the most discrimination then other religious groups; the coverage of Muslims and Islam is relentlessly negative' (Hewstone and Schmid, 2014, p.321).

Racism undermines people's confidence and sense of belonging, and breaks down community cohesion. The girls in the writing group discussed in this book often felt that they were under attack, and they write about the home being a place of sanctuary as the outside world becomes hostile towards Muslim girls.

People of ethnic minority backgrounds may become unsure of their place in society and find themselves asking: 'Where do I belong?'. There was a sense of false hope that we had eradicated racism in our society, but it was always there bubbling away under the surface. As Leah (1995) argues, 'racism is part of our reality, it never goes away, it's under our skin, it's with us all the time' (p.16). Sadly we did not see recent events, such as the American election result, Brexit and the rise in Islamophobia, coming. Ward (2004) rightly argues that: 'In Britain, the politics of racism have often been a function of defining a particular form of exclusion and racialised Britishness' (p.127). He adds that this narrative of extremist politics has adhered to the slogan used by the National Front in the 1960s: 'There ain't no black in the Union Jack' (Gilroy, 1987). The Far Right narrative creates fear and moral panic in communities, which then ignites fuels of hatred once again. Stanley Cohen (2011), in *Folk devils and moral panic*, argued that: 'Societies are subject, every now and then to period of moral panic; a condition, episode, person or group of persons emerges to become defined as a threat to societal values and interests' (p.1).

There is increasing concern about the rise in United Kingdom Independence Party (UKIP) membership and more Far Right demonstrations across the UK. There have been 20 protests from Far Right groups in South Yorkshire, and 17 have been in Rotherham, since the publication of the Jay Report in 2014[1] (Lockley and Ismail, 2016, p.3). New racist groups use social media to play on people's emotions and vulnerabilities. There is no longer the need for them to stand outside school gates and give out leaflets, as they did in the 1970s, or use football for racist violence. When I was a child, football match days were frightening experiences for me. If I close my eyes, I can still see the imagery of racism, the skinheads, with their Dr Martens boots, dark-wash jeans with cuffs rolled up, covered in swastika tattoos, and the chanting of abuse as they walked by my house. While working on the 'Imagine' project, and during the recent period of regular Far Right marches in Rotherham, I wrote about my childhood experience of football days:

> Saturday was footy day. Skinheads with black boots ready to give a good kicking but not to the ball. Swastika tattoos and vile words printed on their bodies; trouble had arrived.
>   The 'hate army' marches down our street. 'Pakis Out, Out' they shout walking towards the football ground, to this day those words ring in my ear.

Challenging racism through arts-based methodologies

The same co-production and arts-based methodologies that engage communities, methodologies which we advocate for in this book, can also help communities to build coping and resilience mechanisms to combat racism. There is a long tradition of using art and writing to combat racism by women. According to bell hooks, art served a political function, 'Whatever African-Americans created in music, dance, poetry, and painting, it was regarded as testimony, bearing witness, challenging racist thinking' (hooks, 1995, p.66).

The Caribbean-American feminist and civil rights activist Audre Lorde writes: 'We are Black women born in to a society of entrenched loathing and contempt for whatever is Black and female. We are strong and enduring, we are also deeply scared' (Lorde and Clark, 2007, p.8). Stow (2003) notes the power of writing as a way to address racism, arguing that: 'personal narratives become creative outlets for the expression of Black women's thoughts and emotions' (p.59).

This book offers examples of the way in which our community writing groups helped women, young and old, from different backgrounds, including from Afghanistan, Iran, Pakistan and British Muslims, to cope with racism in Rotherham. The writing groups described in this book built the confidence of their female participants to challenge racism and not to accept it as normal and as something that they have to put up with. The girls' writing group drew inspiration from Black American women civil rights activists and other role models that challenged the status quo.

Writing was one avenue for the girls to articulate what was happening in their town. The English Defence League (EDL) is a racist organisation, whose main activity is street demonstrations against the Muslim community. One participant of the girls' group writes about the impact of Far Right marches on her and on her Rotherham community:

EDL don't belong in Rotherham

Rotherham is my home and I like living here and every time the 'Army of Hate' visits us they leave our community feeling vulnerable, the police have enough to deal with, without this unnecessary pressure added.

The EDL's[2] motto is 'Not racist, not violent, and no longer silent'. Does anybody else see the irony in this? 'Not racist.' EDL is a fascist group who are clearly Islamophobic; they are not silent when they are hurling racial abuse. Most Muslims in Rotherham respect the law and want to live peacefully if EDL allow us.

I write this sitting at home as EDL have disrupted another Saturday and create tension between communities long after they are gone, which hardly seems fair. ('Lucy' [pseudonym], aged 16)

The only way the Far Right ideology will triumph is if we sit back and do nothing. Bringing people together in one place at one given time can do a lot to undermine the hatred left behind in towns and cities by the Far Right demonstrations. Getz (2010) states that 'festivals celebrate community values, ideology, identity and continuity' (p.8), and further argues that 'festivals are connected to culture and place, giving each identity and helping bind people to their community'. We must keep celebrating diversity at every opportunity and not let prejudice divide us. Elizabeth Campbell, one of the editorial collective for this book, expressed it best when she said: 'Great moments often come out of moments of despair' (10 November 2016, Skype call).

This book is a chance to advocate for a greater change in the way policies impact on communities, at a time when it is vital for voices from diverse communities to be heard. As collaborative research partners, community members, academics and policy makers, we have a social and ethical responsibility to challenge racist and oppressive views and to engage with communities under attack. Now more than ever, contested communities need effective policy making. This book offers examples of community-based projects that utilise collaborative ethnography, co-production and arts practice methodologies to put community voices at the forefront of knowledge production.

It is important that further investment is put into working with young people and communities, so that collaborative projects such as 'Imagine' can create a long-term positive social impact on divided communities and help to build more cohesive communities that challenge racist ideology. If cohesion is going to be a policy priority, it is important that the work is adequately resourced. We see more and more youth and community provision closing down. Further investment will be needed, to work with young people and communities, and to rebuild a cohesive community that challenges today's racist ideologies and threats.

The following piece of writing by a young woman in Rotherham is a message of hope for the future – one that we can all work towards together:

Living on my street
My street is a very long street. It is very multi-cultural.
On my street live English, Irish, Pakistanis, Scottish, Indian, African, Afghans, Italian, Polish, Slovakians and Spanish
It's good to meet and mix with other people, and learn about each other,
We all get on with each other.
We don't argue.
We accept everyone.
My street is the best street in Rotherham.

Notes
[1] The Independent Inquiry into Child Sexual Exploitation in Rotherham (1997–2013).
[2] www.hopenothate.org.uk/hate-groups/edl.

Part Two
Community histories

THREE

Introducing Rotherham

Kate Pahl and Miles Crompton

Here, we offer a pen-portrait of Rotherham, not as a 'typical' town, but as a town that resides in people's memories, in their lived experience and includes their futures. Places draw people together through communities of interest and deep-seated and historically located collective identities. Making sense of place involves making sense of different communities as well as cultures and histories.

We consulted the literature on community studies to make sense of Rotherham as a place, but we also draw on the voices in this book and the oral histories we have collected, as well as visual representations and poetry. This book focuses more specifically on the lived experience of people living in Rotherham. The book is written by people who live in Rotherham as well as those who live outside Rotherham and, in some cases, in countries other than the UK. We do, however, argue that people living in the communities under discussion (and in this case, Rotherham), have key and insightful research insights to offer the field, which may challenge 'traditional' representations of communities.

We aim to sketch out Rotherham as a remembered place, where people hold knowledge and experiences. It is also a place in the future. This book explores ways in which communities can be represented differently in an age of uncertainty and austerity. We focus on creativity and the arts as a source of hope and a way of imagining better communities. This draws on the central purpose of the 'Imagine' project.[1] As part of the 'Imagine' project, we created a series of interlinked projects within Rotherham, exploring common everyday cultures, writing in the community, artistic images of Rotherham, and oral histories of Rotherham. This book has developed from that project.

Our book is interdisciplinary and this introduction reflects our different disciplines – Kate draws on literary theory and social anthropology, and Miles on social theory and town and regional planning. We write it as a conversation between people, but drawing on other sections of the book to provide an introduction both to the book and to Rotherham. We recognise that our work is multi-voiced and multifaceted, and this is partly our intention in writing this chapter.

When we began to think about Rotherham, we started by thinking about the past and the different ways people held memories of Rotherham. We considered how Rotherham had been represented in the past – through oral histories, through sociological accounts and through historical accounts. However, we also consulted literature on community and on post-industrial communities in particular. We thought about methodologies for understanding space and place. We explored the different ways there are to represent a place. Miles represents places in statistics and in pen-portraits, one of which is represented here. Kate has used objects and stories as a form of representation.[2] She has worked with artists to reshape representational practices in communities and to represent place differently (Pahl, 2014).

Making sense of communities involves making sense of culture. Recognising that 'culture is ordinary' from Raymond Williams (1958, 1989), we consider the role of culture as the way in which people make sense of their lives. We draw on a tradition of community studies (for example Charles and Crow, 2012; Crow and Mah, 2012; Somerville, 2016) to make sense of communities. We argue here that representation by communities, for communities, has to be an important feature of all community studies. The role of the arts – poetry, song, image and story – also needs to be recognised as an equally valid form of knowledge production. This book aims to focus on the voices of community members and the arts and humanities as a way of thinking about communities. This work has to incorporate diversity and difference. Our focus here is on lived experience, and on the way in which the past is understood within the present, through history, through the culture, through experience. Communities are refracted through voices, and these are necessarily diverse, disparate and multiple.

Our intention is to situate Rotherham as a place, both real and as it is represented in sociological, philosophical, artistic and literary writing. Drawing on Miles' experience in policy and research at Rotherham council since 2005 and Kate's ethnographic experience in Rotherham since 2006, we present an account that is familiar to many places.

There are many ways in which places can be studied. Disciplines such as geography, history, urban and regional planning, and sociology have been used to look at communities in different ways. Maps provide one insight into a community, while historical insights provide another. Interviews and focus groups can develop understandings through people's voices about their social worlds, while oral histories can deepen understandings. Visual methodologies, such as photographs, image-based research, film and sensory methodologies, open up new ways of understanding community (Pink, 2009). Places can be understood through numbers. Some academics use statistics to portray neighbourhoods – these can be combined to form what are called the Indices of Deprivation, which use statistics collected by government to measure poverty, unemployment and education levels to assess neighbourhoods and the challenges they face. These can create deficit discourses of poverty, as neighbourhoods are described as 'deprived' based on income level or low educational qualifications held within the area. While these are undoubtedly important, other factors, such as quality of life, green space, places to play and community spirit, are also important in people's appreciation of where they live.

Places have been represented through studying their social structure, history and stories, exploring, through interviews, family structure, employment patterns and networks. There are many classic examples where one community was repeatedly studied, sometimes revisited, to understand how people in it worked, lived and experienced their lives (for example Willmott and Young, 1957; Pahl, 1984; Charles and Crow, 2012). These involve long-term involvement in a community context, sometimes living in the same place and participating in daily life. 'The Other Side of Middletown' (Lassiter et al, 2004) involved a collaborative ethnographic study with a particular community, of a place. With sociology, initially there was a focus on the 'typical' community, which, in many ways is not necessary; all communities are idiosyncratic, but many underlying patterns, such as de-industrialisation and the relationship between capital and labour, forcing movement or inflicting unemployment, can be found in many similar communities (Charles and Crow, 2012). Baggini (2007) did, however, attempt to find the 'typical English town' and this search, ironically, led to Rotherham, or more specifically, postal district S66, incorporating Bramley, Maltby and Wickersley. Baggini's study of Rotherham was partial, but he did live for one year in Bramley and his book *Welcome to Everytown* quirkily celebrates his experience of 'ordinary' England.

To find out about places, anthropologists have often gone on walks. Visual anthropologists have taken photographs, sociologists have conducted interviews and focus groups, and historians have conducted oral histories and studied archives. Geographers have made maps and explored the imaginaries of place and space (Massey, 2005). Archaeologists have conducted digs, poets have drawn on the language of the everyday, and song-writers have made up songs about the past, present and future. Artists have represented communities in visual ways, as well as engaging with communities in arts projects that have a common purpose (Kester, 2004). Communities have been represented through the eyes of children (Christensen and O'Brien,

2003) or in sensory and embodied ways (Pink, 2009). Walking tours through communities, where people have felt and experienced things differently, have created access to different ways of knowing and feeling about communities (Vergunst, 2010). Understanding communities through the eyes of people who live there has led to the production of artistic modes of enquiry, such as film, visual arts or literary texts. Our attempt to represent Rotherham in this book has drawn on oral histories and document analysis, but also engagement with the arts as a form of knowing and as a way of understanding reality that lets in other kinds of experience and knowing.

We can make sense of a place through feeling it, and learning about it as an imaginary space. A community can be understood through its past, its migration patterns and through archival records and oral histories. Recording the pathways and shops in a community can be done through visual methodologies, but also as a process of 'coming to know' through community histories, stories and conceptualisations. The process of knowing a community can be done through capturing lived experiences and ways of knowing that are historically and geographically located, but that can also be found in the mind and in the imagination. Ways of knowing that echo people's lived experience are often the best way to find out about communities.

Remembering Rotherham

The way that we began finding out about Rotherham on the 'Imagine' project was to conduct oral histories, in which people told stories of the past, and of their memories of the 1960s and 1970s. In many of these histories, people from Rotherham described how neighbours shared food and literacy practices and people helped each other out with forms and money. These described an experience of collectivity and collective identities that we identified as being important for a sense of place.

Rotherham grew rapidly following the Industrial Revolution, experienced deep and profound changes that created an industrial community, which then had to adapt to changes brought about by outside forces. De-industrialisation led to high levels of unemployment and poverty in the 1980s, some of which has proved difficult to shift over the last thirty years. Despite this, there are positive things about Rotherham that we want to highlight in this book and our intention is to provide a 'counter narrative' to the often depressing accounts of Rotherham in the press, and in particular in the Jay Report (Jay, 2014).[3] This report drew attention to a wider culture of not listening to women and girls within Rotherham. The report also made reference to many of the abusers being of Pakistani heritage, which had the effect of heightening already tense race relations, and led to a number of marches by extreme right-wing groups in the town. The Jay Report, in August 2014, did have a strong effect on our research. Our book has come about partly in order to respond to this experience and labelling of Rotherham, to provide a more positive account for the future that acknowledges that these events took place but also focuses on creating new and positive visions of the future.

Memories of places can involve a nostalgic calling up of past remembered freedoms, of playing out or of harsh experiences of racism and exclusion. Childhood is when memories are laid down and become told and retold. The same stories often emerged when we conducted oral histories. People remembered their experiences of the tin bath, the Singer sewing machine, the outside toilet, and how mothers slipped on the ice while pregnant going up the garden path, the smell of food and the feel of lining up while hair was plaited and breakfast was got ready and the fire was lit. These experiences shaped and structured the experience of place.

The external environment in the 1960s was also very different – Rotherham's steelworks were fully operating and coal mines ringed the town, all with large workforces. Memories of smoke and clanking trains, the clang of the steelworks and the dirt of the mines emerged as the sound, smell and feel of an industrial community. Many of the men from the British Asian communities worked in the tougher jobs in the steelworks and experienced hardship in their conditions and long working days. Memories rested upon the structure of the days, the set times at which people went to work and the different but shared ways in which women and children lived collective, structured lives.

Memories were both positive and negative. Charlesworth (2000), writing in the 1990s, painted a particularly acute picture of Rotherham as 'a place in which life is consumed by the ordinary everyday mundanity of a people who are excluded from anything approximating to a form of civil society' (p. 25). In Charlesworth's bleak vision, Rotherham is a place of social suffering, and there were very few chinks of hope in his account of the embodied suffering of the poor. In our research, however, many memories were of solidarity and fun, hilarity and 'playing out' in the long summer evenings: 'I remember in the summer holidays playing out until 10 o'clock on the streets ...' (oral history, Rotherham, 2014).

Making sense of a place means thinking historically. It also means working with the people who live in communities, in order to frame ways of thinking that come from lived experience. We think that it is important to talk to and listen to communities. Some of these stories are sad, some joyful, but all are located in the everyday. One feature common to many of the histories we heard was of a sense of collective identities, which had been lost over time. There is a long history of discussions about the relationship between social class, community and feelings of collectivity. Seabrook, writing in the 1980s, noted: 'A certain retreat from community, the faltering, in large sections of the working class, of commitment to collective values, the withering, not of the outer forms but of the very roots of solidarity itself' (Seabrook, 1984, p.4).

Many people in Rotherham who we worked with and who have contributed to this book, or who talked to us as part of the project, were attached to it as a place, even though they were aware that it got negative press. This echoed the experience of Lisa McKenzie in St Ann's in Nottingham (McKenzie, 2015) and Lindsey Hanley in Birmingham (Hanley, 2007). People in Rotherham told stories about their past shared experiences and positive, happy memories, despite experiencing a negative connotation when they explained where they lived to people from outside the place. There was also an underlying sense of pride.

Community futures can be shaped by an understanding of the past, and we found that history and memory were important for the future as well as the past (Siebers and Fell, 2012). 'Community' is a word on the move. Crow and Mah (2012) argue that, 'communities continue to evolve in theory and in practice' (p.4) and recognise that the concept of community has always been contested and under discussion. One of the tasks of the 'Imagine' project was to imagine better communities and make them happen. Our initial work was to think about the role of memory and nostalgia in creating collective memories. Sometimes these were very idealistic, evoking past idylls. For example, from a series of interviews conducted in 2006 for the 'Every object tells a story' project[4], memories emerged that tapped into these visions, and people talked of harmonious race relations and peaceful co-existence:

> Well I can't really say 60s, early 70s really, there was Asians here, there were Asians in the streets ... But it was alright, it was OK, there wasn't any problems, people just lived, you know, people lived whereas now people don't live so easily - or so it seems. (JK, oral history, Rotherham, 2006)

In the 'Imagine' project, poetry, visual art and oral history methodologies were used to explore the meanings of community and of growing up in Rotherham. While some descriptions of Rotherham were negative, we found expressions of hope that were inspiring. For example, the poem at the end of Chapter Two by a young woman from Rotherham describes an equally harmonious depiction of life in Rotherham today, in a diverse street landscape. As a counter to this, descriptions of hardship and difficulty in the 1960s were regularly told as exemplars of 'how much better it is now':

> … mum was saying in the evening we'd clear out the fire and then we'd have the firelighters, wood and the coal ready for the first person that got up in the morning would light the fire. Because she often tells us stories about how difficult it was. (RK, oral history, Rotherham, 2006)

Everyday routines, such as filling the tin bath full of hot water or lighting the coal fire, were described by people as being entwined within the fabric of everyday life. People shared food up and down the street. The sharing of food was also cross-cultural – people remembered sharing food with neighbours of different ethnic backgrounds as part of a culture of support. A core theme of communitarianism, and a focus on shared interests and values, is often a focus of community cohesion policy, but sometimes lacks meaning when it is empty or without value (Robinson, 2008). In our research, sharing of food and past experiences from the 1960s such as the tin bath and the Singer sewing machine, created reservoirs from which communities could locate collective identities. These identities could become a common core around which people could celebrate shared values.

One core way in which people experienced collective identities was through industrialisation. Rotherham was shaped by industrialisation followed by de-industrialisation and changing economic conditions. When we looked at the history of Rotherham, we found that the pattern was of expansion followed by gradual decline as the pits and steelworks faced closure. Up until the middle of the 19th century, Rotherham was a small market town, surrounded by a large rural hinterland that included agricultural villages. When a pit was opened, this transformed those communities almost overnight. Rotherham went through huge changes in the late Industrial Revolution, which shaped the character of the town. The development of coal mines happened at a later stage than some of the other British coalfields, such as Durham or South Wales, mainly because the coal seams were deeper.

The Rotherham coal mines were largely opened in the latter part of the Industrial Revolution. As a result, there was immense population growth between 1890 and 1910. Rotherham and surrounding villages continued to grow until the mid-1980s. People came from other parts of the UK and from Ireland, to work in the pits and steelworks. In the 1960s and early 1970s people came from Pakistani-administered Kashmir and also from Yemen to work in the steel industry.

This led to a very particular experience for people in Rotherham, who grew up in the 1960s and 1970s with secure employment, only to see their jobs and the foundations of the local economy vanish with the closures of the 1980s. People in Rotherham experienced unprecedented growth of industrial activity in coal and steel followed by a long period of gradual change, culminating in dramatic closures. The steel and coal mining industries were big employers, typically over a thousand people worked in a single coal mine and a steelworks usually employed several thousand. The mines in Rotherham were big and continued to expand underground or merge with others until their closure. The effect of this rapid expansion and dominance was that people's lives revolved around the pits and steelworks.

The demographics of Rotherham include a large concentration of Pakistani and Kashmiri heritage families, mostly from the Mirpur region, following settlement in the 1960s. Some of the areas of early Kashmiri settlement, particularly Eastwood and Ferham, now host a sizeable and growing Slovak Roma community. Smaller communities include Polish, Irish and Black African communities that, in some cases, have become absorbed within the wider communities. There is also a growing group of dual- or multiple-heritage children and young people born to people marrying across cultures. Most minority ethnic communities in Rotherham have young and growing populations, but at the same time, Pakistani heritage families are experiencing deaths from within the first generation, who migrated to Rotherham in the 1960s and 1970s. While central Rotherham is ethnically diverse, most of the borough beyond two miles from the town centre is effectively monocultural in terms of ethnicity.

The embodied and visceral experiences of industrialisation were vividly described by Charlesworth (2000), who produced an image of Rotherham as 'scarred' by the collective devastation of coal mining as a practice and then de-industrialisation, creating: 'simply devastation, the largest areas of industrial dereliction in Europe' (p.33). Charlesworth's depiction is unremittingly bleak; however, the collective nature of experience did mean that public services and ways of doing things were shared. Transportation systems reflected this collective world, in which public transport was well connected to the coal mines and steelworks, so that workers could reach their jobs. Coal and steel were moved by rail, and workers usually travelled by bus to the pits. People followed the work in the pits, often starting work in a neighbouring village, but when the pit closed down, they would transfer to another mine. The Dearne Valley and Rotherham were hubs of transportation of coal and steel rather than of passengers.

Within the coal mining villages, enduring family and wider social bonds were created and reinforced. There were strong social bonds between people across generations. The effect of de-industrialisation was to divide communities. Rotherham became increasingly divided after the early 1980s, both in relation to the aftermath of the miners' strike but also in relation to lived experience. The experience of working down the pits or in steelworks united communities, but it was hard to understand the experience of losing a livelihood so suddenly, and outsiders struggled to understand the culture of working in coal mining. One of the most problematic phrases from the 1980s was Norman Tebbit's much publicised (and often misquoted) comment, 'I grew up in the '30s with an unemployed father. He didn't riot. He got on his bike and looked for work, and he kept looking till he found it'[5]. For people living in relatively isolated communities with close-knit families in places like the Dearne Valley and Rotherham, this was insulting but also, this expression did not recognise the 'structure of feeling' (Williams 1958/1989) that people lived within. Coal and steel were a way of life as well as production industries. People spent their lives together, in the workplace and outside in the community, fostering a strong collective culture. Varied employment opportunities in recent decades have provided new jobs, but cannot act as a substitute for the collective culture of the industries that they replaced.

These collective bonds were never acknowledged within the ideologies of Thatcherism, which sought to destroy concepts of the social collective. This led to a sense of loss and an experience of 'social haunting' (Bright, 2012). This articulated the feelings of injustice and anger that were often found just beneath the surface in some of the hardest-hit areas of Rotherham. The legacy of de-industrialisation in Rotherham was a nostalgic longing for a time when community bonds were strong and collective experiences created shared memories and identities. These were often translated into a fear of outsiders and shared perceptions of 'otherness' that sometimes led to a fear of migrants and strangers coming from out of town. Such attitudes were reflected in the local vote to leave the European Union in June 2016, which was often articulated in Rotherham as being about preventing new migrants from coming to the town. Large-scale, EU-funded regeneration programmes benefiting South Yorkshire over many years failed to generate a positive image of the organisation. Another aspect of this was the need to return in the imagination to a place that celebrated those values of community, solidarity and cohesion.

Understanding Rotherham

Understanding Rotherham therefore means listening to community knowledge, and considering ways of thinking about communities. Our vision in this book is for people to locate themselves within their own histories. We have alluded earlier to oral histories that we have done, which located people's experiences of life in Rotherham in a specific time and place. We were able to identify patterns and ways of doing things that were common to many communities in Rotherham, including strong family bonds, people rooted in local areas, and a need to stay within particular streets and areas. People 'got by': supporting each other with skills such as filling in forms, cooking, providing help with small repairs and finding someone in the neighbourhood who knew how to help.

Community participation also includes civic engagement. Civic engagement is growing within the Pakistani heritage community, as Zanib Rasool (see Chapter Thirteen in this volume) describes. While many new migrants are still focused on finding work, voluntarism and civic pride are being fostered within communities. Miles Crompton referenced surveys for the council in order to find out what people liked about Rotherham. While community cohesion has recently been highlighted as a concern within Rotherham, when surveyed on what they liked about Rotherham, people liked the open spaces, the parks and the green spaces.

While Rotherham's media image continues to concern many people, in everyday life people walk their dogs, exchange greetings with their neighbours, carry out litter picks and send their children to schools that work hard to support young people's aspirations and wellbeing. It is important to consider who is defining the story and how the story is told. We can provide accounts of post-industrial devastation, or we can listen to children and young people define their worlds themselves, telling stories that might contain elements of hope, resistance, beauty, rebellion or contemplation (Pahl, 2014; Pool and Pahl, 2015).

In this book, we consider what happens when personal constructions of community and identity are brought to the fore, and people tell the story themselves. While the landscape of industrial decline has shaped Rotherham, we want to counter the often negative accounts of the town with a new energy of renewal that is focused more on the arts, on lived experience and on the everyday as a locus for thinking. This is our argument for co-production as a methodology; it lets in new voices and also new modes of inquiry. The book we present, as we explain in Chapter One, is multi-voiced. It does not present a 'definitive' view of Rotherham; it is partial and committed, with a focus on hopeful futures.

In writing this chapter, we have had many conversations. As a university academic and a town planner, we bring different perspectives. Both of us are outsiders to Rotherham, but we share a commitment to the place. We like talking to people and we are interested in learning about the world around us, Kate as an ethnographer and Miles as a town planner. We like to learn from communities, and from people who are able to provide contextual information from lived experience. This knowledge is rich, diverse and important for policy makers.

Notes

[1] This project, 'Imagine', was a five-year funded programme that looked at the social, historical, cultural and democratic context of civic engagement, with a focus on imagining better communities and making them happen. Funded by the UK's Economic and Social Research Council, the project was also developed through the Connected Communities programme, which had an aim to support research that was developed with, not on, communities. ESRC Grant number: ES/K002686/2.

[2] See: www.everyobjecttellsastory.org.uk.

[3] See the Jay Report (2014), which was a Council-sponsored investigation into child sexual exploitation in the town (www.rotherham.gov.uk/downloads/file/1407/independent_inquiry_cse_in_rotherham). The substantive content of the report was an investigation into why a large number of young people, mainly girls, were systematically sexually abused over a period of years (1997-2013).

[4] See: www.everyobjecttellsastory.org.uk.

[5] See: https://en.wikipedia.org/wiki/Norman_Tebbit.

FOUR

How can historical knowledge help us to make sense of communities like Rotherham?

Elizabeth Pente and Paul Ward

What counts for knowledge?

What counts as historical knowledge is controlled by powerful forces. In establishing a new national curriculum for history, Michael Gove, education secretary in David Cameron's Conservative government between 2010 and 2014 (Paton, 2010), favoured a broadly chronological account of Britain's story, with children being taught about Britain's impact on the world. This was a response to critiques by the political Right, who wanted a set of 'facts' about Britain to be taught, rather than the historical skills that enabled children to understand their own place in history.

The Better History Group (a short-lived, right-wing group of teachers) argued in 2010 that: 'we believe that the teaching of British history has been allowed to deteriorate, to such an extent that substantial numbers of young people do not have that basic grasp of this country's history that they need in order to function as informed and active adult citizens' (Paton, 2010). The phrase 'this country's history' was considered unproblematic – an account of what constitutes knowledge being related to the history of great men and the occasional great woman, rather than connecting to ordinary people's lives.

After some pressure, campaigners secured the inclusion of Mary Seacole, the Jamaican-born Black woman, who nursed British soldiers in the Crimean War (1853-56) in the list of topics for history teaching on the national curriculum (Rawlinson, 2013). This success marked an important point in understanding ethnic diversity in British history and recognising that ordinary people wanted a say in what counts as historical knowledge. But history teaching often relies on what happens in universities. In academic history, traditionally, historians study the past as 'lone scholars', as individual historians who formulate research questions, conduct research in libraries and archives and then write sole-authored academic outputs. Therefore, what usually counts for knowledge is single-authored books and journal articles produced by professional historians. Historians in universities then privilege writing by other historians in universities as they develop their thinking about the past.

This study of history writing is called 'historiography', and it forms the basis of what university students are taught on their degree programmes. The problem with this process is that it is quite exclusive. It limits what counts for historical knowledge to what is written in universities. It can limit the scope of knowledge produced and the range of history studied, in part because in Britain, at least, university historians come from fairly narrow social backgrounds. They also tend to favour national and international history over local histories. Yet at a local level, issues of class, gender and ethnicity are played out in people's everyday lives. If historians don't research histories that matter to ordinary people, then what is taught in schools is likely to remain limited.

There have been changes in the way in which history has been researched. The subfields of oral, community and public history have evolved over recent decades – and so have the products of historical research. These subdisciplines work with people outside universities to explore a broader range of knowledge, working with people to tell their own histories, which are often locally based and which reveal ethnic diversity. Additionally, universities are placing more emphasis on academics engaging with 'the public' and showing the relevance of research to society. There is still an emphasis on academics producing peer-reviewed books and articles, but what counts for knowledge is expanding, although hesitantly.

This is essential, given the importance of history in developing a sense of identity and community. People are products of their experience, and communities are products of collective experience over time – communities emerge from their history, as do the places in which they live. Approached in this way, history can provide a sense of belonging even to the newest arrivals. The focus in these chapters in this book is on Rotherham but, as a way of working, the methods are transferable to other localities and communities as well.

How do we make historical knowledge?

One of the ways in which historians are expanding what counts for knowledge is by adopting methodologies of co-production (Lloyd and

Moore, 2015). Co-production of research can be defined at its most basic as research *with* people rather than *on* people. The co-production of historical knowledge involves partnerships between academic historians and public groups or individuals, who bring expertise born of their experiences, to undertake historical research using primary source materials (Ward and Pente, 2017). Co-production brings marginalised and/or alternative histories to the fore, and makes them 'count' as valued knowledge.

Examples of community-based historical research can be seen in Heritage Lottery funded schemes, such as 'All Our Stories' and 'First World War: Then and Now'. Both schemes encourage community groups to work with universities to develop historical research skills. Both have encouraged a tremendously wide range of projects that reflect varieties of ethnic diversity in the exploring the past. 'All Our Stories' included projects by Gypsies in Derbyshire, on Black people in Tudor England and on working-class people in a factory in Leicester (HLF, 2015).

Similarly, the centenary of the First World War has been much more diverse because of the community-based research enabled by the HLF and supported by the Arts and Humanities Research Council through the World War One Engagement Centres, including the Centre for Hidden Histories, which has 'a particular interest in the themes of migration and displacement, the experience of "others" from countries and regions within Europe, Asia and the Commonwealth, the impact and subsequent legacies of the war on diverse communities within Britain, remembrance and commemoration, and identity and faith' (Centre for Hidden Histories, 2014).

Why does it matter?

What counts as historical knowledge is transformed when people are placed at the centre of the research process. Histories of Rotherham blossom into histories of global significance through an exploration of the intersections between the local – histories of our street and our house – and the rest of the world, through questions of mobility and movement. Rotherham exported coal and steel to the world and, in return, it was enriched by inward migration.

We hope that the historical chapters in this book (Chapters Three to Ten) raise some questions for readers to consider. We suggest that the notion of 'organic intellectuals' from Antonio Gramsci could be used to think about how communities contain organic historians – people who are interested in the past as a tool to change the future. Gramsci was a socialist imprisoned in Fascist Italy in the 1930s. He suggested that 'traditional intellectuals' were the philosophers, artists and historians who perform a specific intellectual function that emphasises continuity in society to manufacture consent for existing social relations.

We think that the co-production of research – and the development of new digital media – presents a challenge. It enables the emergence of organic intellectuals, who 'think and act elsewhere and in other ways than the traditional intellectual' (Organon, no date; see also Lacy, 2014). Some 'organic intellectuals' are not progressive (so, for example in Chapter Six, Pente and Ward discuss YouTube and comments 'below the line' that rail against change in British society), but others challenge ideas of continuity and hold out possibilities for change. For example, Virsa, a bhangra dance group based in Huddersfield, argue that their research on histories of the Panjabi dance is about 'celebrating our past, preserving our future' (Virsa, no date). In Rotherham, Tassibee, a partner organisation in the 'Imagine' project, worked with Pakistani girls to '"Imagine" better futures', but the focus of their project was 'to explore how cultural times have changed over the generations'. Tassibee and the participating girls became their own, organic, historians.

This raises the question of who is a historian. It also raises questions about where documents and artefacts of history are located and stored. Traditionally this has been in archives, but we might ask what is – and what is not – in the archive? What do the presence and absence of particular historical records reveal about what is valued in the past? How can communities address the absences of their histories, through different kinds of family and community histories, including art and other creative outputs that capture the present for future archives? Answering these questions is likely to contribute to a different sense of history.

FIVE

Some poems, a song and a prose piece

Ray Hearne and Ryan Bramley

Ray Hearne: I have chosen pieces not published elsewhere but which remain representative of my work since the millennium, i.e. a continuing sequence of writings wrestling with my attempts, as the child of immigrants, to define my sense of South Yorkshireness. From rural Catholic Ireland to Parkgate, a steel community, surrounded by chimneys, engirdled by collieries. A people defined by their labour in heavy industries, living in landscapes scorched, ravaged and degraded, speaking their own variants of a language scoffed at by the arbiters of good English. I kind of loved it. Written in the last few years the poems try to articulate the smoke-choked experience of the 1960s and 1970s.

Ryan Bramley: As a small boy, I grew up at the fringe of the world: Thurnscoe. I sat in the borough of Barnsley, with a Sheffield postcode and a Rotherham phone code; and yet, my little red terraced-house seemed closer to Doncaster than anything else. It set the tone for life to be lived on the periphery, and that's where my poem in this chapter finds itself: in a contested space between working-class pride, and middle-class aspiration; between belonging and rootlessness. The piece I have written centres on a large village called Wath-Upon-Dearne (or, as my lot at home used to say, 'Waff-on-Dearne'), and how its former grammar-school-turned-comprehensive has long been heralded as one of South Yorkshire's brighter beacons of education – not because it teaches people how to value

Rotherham, or Barnsley, or Doncaster, as home;
but because it equips budding young students with
the tools required to leave this place for good. And
in my eyes, that's a great shame.

The film of the book of the film

A library of rare unwritten books,
Park Gaters; always at it, day and night,
priceless plot and character, whole epics
to be made of angel, giant, troglodyte.

"The dirtiest place in Europe" we could boast;
that hyperbolic trope from some telly feature
gave us a kind of identity, though the cost
we knew was stuntedness, it gave us stature.

Perverse it may have been but we were proud,
equal to the loud steel, the crafty coal,
those chains of chimneys, voluble and crude,
the slag itself choking our childish souls,

the three-shift treadmill's timeless clock-machine;
men whose darkened laughter never saw print,
women eclipsed by walls of washing-line,
even in the poem's light, still at their stint.

Ray Hearne

See amid the winter snow

Landslips of waste, combustible desolation
Coal Board detritus, extemporised willy-nilly
Stinks that sang our epics of slagscape, brimstone
And old dogmas ingested less than critically

Scorched earth of an altar-boy's smutted youth
Awe and terror like ores seaming my heart
The smoulder of dreams, and local versions of truth
That parodied anything more subtle than the knuckler's art

Sky-lines of smoke-spoor, pit-yard emergencies
Nothing but so much grit in the oyster-shell
Of some gob-fire boiling within me, whose urgencies
Like incantations loom in their lustre still.

Shove a stick in a spoil-heap and pull it out burning
My flaming pen would set thick air on fire
Blazing its trail for Don and Rother yearning
Above and beyond all our mountained up Low End mire.

Ray Hearne

Mangham Lane

A street of wheezing houses and a chemical works
whose potent influences fell upon us daily;
ashes on our lungs, dusts on our childish songs,
the efficacious whiff, a stench, a tang
defining our tastes, traces veining our tongues.

A sentimental alchemy beguiled;
what killed us forged our hearts of mythic gold.

Ray Hearne

Guest and Chrimes 1972

When I was nineteen I went for a job at Guest and Chrimes. In those days it was the biggest foundry in Rotherham and had been so for more than a century. It stood on Don Street just beyond the centre of town, across from the fairground where the 'Stattis,' the statutes fair, came twice yearly. I had worked already on gas pipelines with my dad and his navvy mates, I had sweated in steelworks with concrete-gangs and furnace wreckers, I had barrowed bricks on building sites, I was fit, strong; ten ton; ready for anything. The interview was straightforward; could I start the following Monday? A foreman led me out of the office to show me my new place of work. It was the smell, even in the yard, that struck me first; that tincture of something burnt, scalded, roasted and scorched, all at the same time, with an occasional dark chocolate acidity that tickled the back of the throat.

He took me through the doors and into the foundry itself. I was unprepared for the experience, horrendous intense heat, small furnaces seemingly at every corner. I recall no windows, no air to breathe. The shop-floor was littered with piles of what looked like dark sand; little smouldering heaps. Muscular men in tattered vests dripping with sweat, hands engulfed in big thick gauntlets, heaved huge metallic moulds around the place. My bottle went. I could not get out fast enough. I remember saying to myself, 'Dante's Inferno.'

At that time I hadn't yet read the poem but I'd seen an extract from the film. How could anyone spend a life of such toil in such conditions? From that moment Guest and Chrimes came to represent to me Rotherham's hellish underworld; forever present, seething away at its core in perpetual civic heartburn. In that spirit, right up to today, I have never ceased to incubate my own incipient sense of the price paid by some for economic survival.

Ray Hearne

First childhood
What were they trying to say
those big chimneys
open-mouthed and chuntering
around my cot?
Ranged huge against our skies
like the ogling dead
chanting their mumbo-jumbo,

shadowers over shared yards
hearts in magniloquent gobs
what were they saying?
Craning the lengths of their necks
like awkward uncles at a wake
pitching way above my head
some indecipherable blather;

steel-plant, forge, Chemics,
simultaneous bellowings
spittling the day's petals

and every cloud had a sulphur lining;
fallout on a Whitsun shirt,
smutty hieroglyphs smeared
across sheets pegged out too long;

bombast or benediction
that monotone of motes
waffling down from on high
to colonise every bone,
the very lungs of our dreams?
I swallowed it all whole
till I woke myself up in my sleep.

Forest of brittle beanstalks!
Filthy great trumpeters!
Tall tale spreaders with a vengeance!
All that elevated talk
belittled at last by silence.
Only now in their absence,
playing it by ear always

am I learning how to 'Imagine'
songs in that lost language,
teaching myself to believe
when I hear them again welling,
each voice will be my own,
though I am only telling
you what I was told.

Ray Hearne

We should be singing[1]
In Rotherham Town there's a dark cloud over
The song of steel singer's hearts of gold
High above your scaffolder and roofer
The steeple-toed cockerel's blood runs cold

This is not the song I should be singing
This is not the song I had hoped to sing

It's a darker cloud than the smoke of ages

The smog and muck of the forge and mill
Ferrous fogs we fought, for us bits of wages
And the histories we seem to cling to still

Reports abound and the shock's bewild'rin'
A darker truth than a coal-black sky
For the town's accused of abusing children
And there's 1400 plus reasons why

This is not the song I should be singing
This is not the song I had hoped to sing

There's some in care who were far from cared for
Cultivated, groomed, violated, used
It's a tale of shame we were ill prepared for
In us very midst, who can be excused?

Blame the social workers, and the taxi drivers
The safeguarders' creaky systems too
And the councillors and all the late arrivers
But where the hell was I, and where the hell were you?

This is not the song I should be singing
This is not the song I had hoped to sing

They were someone's sons, daughters, nephews, nieces
A neighbour's grandkids shared around, - who knew?
Brutalised, manhandled, innocence in pieces
And then even blamed by the boys in blue

And it isn't one race or skin complexion
Nor one religion or religion's lack
In a given year, and I'll stand correction
There's more abusers here that's white, than black

This is not the song I should be singing
This is not the song I had hoped to sing

But what kind of un-man or un-human creature
Can yin or yang with a rapist gang?
May each name and face feature, and not in miniature,
Across the front page of the Yorkshire Jang

In Rotherham town every future's tainted
And will remain so until the day
The final perpetrator's decanted
For a twenty year stretch and banged away

This is not the song I should be singing
This is not the song I had hoped to sing

Ray Hearne

Waff-on-Dearne
You'd be hard pushed to find a flame
within this valley of unspent coal,
none burns as bright beyond the blame
which riddles the land of cope-on-dole.
Hope, like the banks of the River Dearne –
once often burst with future thoughts –
now left to toil beneath inertia's
turn: the present Maggie brought.
The post-industrial Yorkshire bairn
stands on watch by Barnsley station,
watching the buses and trains adjourn
to take the folk to any location
but here. Stranded like the old pithead,
the coal-face kid digs up the dead.

Down the road, *Meliora Spectare*:
"Look to Better Things" – like Latin gait
on a Rov'rum school's crest. Translated: *beware
of the kids round 'ere who dun't talk reyt.*
The coal-face kid could never stride
beyond those doors (his head held high)
without the proper code applied:
the shirt, the blazer, the emblem tie.
Dressed for desertion: the highest prize
these kids are told they can receive's
bequest between the printed lines
of one-way ticket for scholar's leave.
*Leave your burning spirit behind
and look to better things.*

Ryan Bramley

Note

1   This song was written in 2016. Any writer associated with Rotherham has to
address somehow the horrors revealed by the child sexual abuse revelations.

SIX

Who are we now? Local history, industrial decline and ethnic diversity

Elizabeth Pente and Paul Ward

In this chapter, we challenge what might be called a 'local history paradigm', whereby immigration to Britain and the decline of industry are linked and local history is considered to 'end' in the 1980s. We explore representations of past and present in Rotherham, and draw on examples of heritage projects undertaken there by people from minority ethnic communities. We consider ways in which these projects add to the local history narrative of the town.

William Gould and Irna Qureshi have explored south Asian histories in Britain in the context of the postcolonial migrant experience, arguing that local histories need to take account of the imperial nature of British history (Gould and Qureshi, 2014). They argue that British south Asian histories are often confined to a local context and do not contribute to national or imperial historiographies. We argue that minority ethnic histories *are not often enough* integrated into 'local history' and so are marginalised at every level of historical research and scholarship, both 'professional' and 'amateur'. We suggest that using methodologies of co-production might link histories of ethnic diversity to histories of locality and community, and that integrated local histories could contribute to a broader national and transnational history. By co-production in history, we mean the interpretation of the past by academically trained historians and public groups, who bring expertise born of experience and emotion, to undertake systematic historical research together using primary sources (Pente et al, 2015). This chapter, like the rest of the book, was the product of a series of writing workshops held in Rotherham involving community and academic partners. It emerged from the experience of many of the participants living in and researching the town during the child sexual exploitation scandal. Nonetheless, while about Rotherham, its interpretation might be applicable to a variety of post-industrial towns and cities in northern England and elsewhere.

Thinking about the past is important. It enables people to locate where they are in the present and to think about the future. People in towns and cities in northern England are constantly engaged in a variety of forms of historical recovery, as they seek to understand their present condition looking back to 'better' times. With massive deindustrialisation having destroyed the coal and steel industries in South Yorkshire, there is a desire to look back past pit and plant closures to see industrialisation in the 19th and early 20th centuries as playing a major role in building communities and constructing class, civic and urban identities. One narrative that emerges from such constructions tends to connect decline and poverty with post-war immigration, from the Indian sub-continent and the West Indies between the 1950s and 1990s and from Eastern Europe since 2004. In some northern cities, long-term and systematic child sexual exploitation, associated with Asian men, though not exclusively carried out by them, has added to a sense of decline of values and morals alongside economic and urban decay. This association has exacerbated the already existent notion of blaming 'immigrants' for the contemporary decline of northern English cities. The 'Brexit' vote in the referendum on membership of the European Union (EU) further encouraged hostility towards immigrants and their descendants, in the context of a belief in an historic shift, in which white Britons would be able to 'take back control' of 'their' country.

The association of immigration with decay and decline has resulted in narratives of the past creating what might be called a 'local history' model. This model privileges positive features of the past, such as the aesthetics of rural landscapes and industrial townscapes, the importance of communities of solidarity in the face of industrial poverty, traditional family life and kinship, education and forms of leisure, embedded in a sense of progress and 'Britishness' associated with the two World Wars. In much of this narrative, history – and often the nation – has been considered to 'come to an end' with the closure of heavy industry and the miners' strike of 1984-85. Such narratives act to exclude newer communities from telling historical stories, downplaying their contribution in the British past as well as in the present and future. This raises questions, relevant globally, about who 'owns' history. Rauna Kuokkanen, drawing on thinking by Gayatri Spivak, explains how academic elite knowledge in universities often forecloses or erases the perspectives of marginalised groups and communities, including indigenous peoples (Kuokkanen, 2008, p.66). We suggest that this process can often be exacerbated, when imposed on immigrant and descendant communities, whose right to reside in a locality is frequently questioned.

Rotherham owed its population growth in the 19th century to its iron and steel industries, coal mining, glass works and the milling of grain (see also Chapter Three). The population of the borough rose from around 17,000 in 1801 to 120,000 in 1901. Even in 1933, during the inter-war depression, Rotherham produced one seventh of Britain's output of steel, which employed 4,250 men (Munford, 2003, p.9). Local historian Anthony Munford considered how iron and steel production meant the formation of football and cricket teams, brass bands, amateur operatic and theatrical societies, the building of chapels and large houses such as Clifton House and Ferham House, and how from this combination of working-class and middle-class culture there emerged a sense of civic duty (Munford, 2003, p.150).

Local history publications across the UK celebrate industrial success, which then compounds the subsequent sense of decline and loss. They also privilege the distant medieval and early modern past as contributing to progress in history leading to the Industrial Revolution. There are three volumes about Rotherham in the 'Aspects of Local History' series published by Wharncliffe. They focus on the pre-industrial age, with chapters on Tudor will-makers, South Yorkshire's aristocratic families, watermills, medieval deer parks, common land, and dovecotes (Jones, 1995, 1996, 2002). There are then chapters on industry, with the development of the railways and lending libraries and steel works. Such books rarely discuss ethnic diversity in the past. Even Arthur Wharton, Britain's first black professional footballer, who played for Rotherham Town FC in the 1890s, is rarely mentioned (Vasili, 1998).

In the consultation undertaken by the borough council in 2015 in the wake of the child sexual exploitation events, people were asked: 'What do you like about Rotherham?'. On the one hand, the report stated that 'positive views were directed at the Minster, Minster Gardens and neighbouring areas of the High Street ... Rotherham's history and heritage were mentioned several times, referencing Wentworth Woodhouse and other historic buildings' (Rotherham Metropolitan Borough Council (RMBC), 2015, p.5). On the other hand, immigration was viewed negatively: 'Immigration and ethnic segregation were seen as major issues in the online survey, with many people expressing strong feelings about immigration generally' (RMBC, 2015, p.6).

A sense of loss has dominated popular readings of Rotherham's history, and it leaks into some academic works. In 2000, Simon Charlesworth described how his book about the town:

> focused upon the town of Rotherham, part of what was once a whole network of interconnecting towns and villages that gave South Yorkshire its distinctive culture. An area that has suffered de-industrialization and the attendant consequences of poverty ... This book ... is an attempt to set down a living record, a testimony to a dying way of life; the extinction of a kind of people. (Charlesworth, 2000, p.1)

The development of popular history on the internet has provided a forum for similar, less evidentially rigorous, interpretations of change and decline. A variety of websites seek to capture and celebrate Rotherham's industrial past. For example, the now defunct rotherhamweb.co.uk drew together a range of historical documents and reminiscences of places in the district – from the Domesday Book to mid-20th century memories of school days, working lives, leisure, places and buildings. The Second World War is a recurrent theme in memories, given its centrality to a sense of British national identity in the post-war period, as Britain's global power and authority have diminished relative to international rivals. The war is largely conceptualised at the local level as the contribution made by the home front, including the munitions produced by local industry, and the communication between soldiers serving overseas and those at home (see, for example, Age Concern Rotherham, 2007).

Such interpretations, providing a requiem for a lost period, have been articulated expansively on YouTube in a pair of films made in 2009 by Darren Flinders (2009a, 2009b). Their titles enunciate loss: 'I remember when Rotherham was good: part one'; and 'I remember when Rotherham was good: part two. When England had an identity'. Both are short collections of still images set to evocative music of loss, such as *Clair de Lune* by Claude Debussy. Most of the images in the first film are from local postcards and include depictions of public houses, street scenes with trams, horse-drawn carts, the cattle market and Rotherham's chantry chapel. The second film consists of Victorian images, such as tollgates and cottages as well as the town centre, the railway station and, in a collapsing of time, images from post-war Rotherham, such as an ice-cream tricycle. The films have had (at the time of writing) about 4,300 and 11,400 views respectively. Part two, particularly, provoked a series of 'below the line' comments, many of which shared the sense of loss evoked in the films, blaming a variety of causes in blunt language. One, from 2015, gathered a variety of causes together:

> I think many of us who see these wonderful old photos of our past mourn the fact that our country has turned to shit!!! Everything that made us the proud nation we once were has been changed/sold off/closed down, who are we now?? and who are the bastards who took our identity. Take a look at Rotherham now, that is the Britian [*sic*] we have left, also, every piece of lowlife terrorist scum we refer to as British is another nail in our coffin, an insult to our ancestors who bequeathed to us a once proud nation, p.s. Rotherham is now famous for the most sickening and coordinated attack on children who are probably related to some of the people in the photos! (Flinders, 2009b, comment by 'dog pound')

Immigration and ethnic diversity have widely been seen as contributing to the decline of the urban north, and the ownership that people feel over their history and destiny is seen as having been weakened by industrial decline. In Rotherham, the collapse of the steel industry and the miners' strike, followed by closure of the last coal mine, when Maltby Main was mothballed in 2012, has resulted in widespread pessimism about the future of the town. The link between child sexual exploitation and minority ethnic communities has been widely asserted and the Jay Report (Jay, 2014) has described how issues of ethnicity affected the handling of child sexual exploitation in Rotherham, with fear of being branded 'racist' preventing decisive action against the perpetrators of abuse (see Miah, 2015).

In Rotherham, pessimism resulted in the election of ten United Kingdom Independence Party (UKIP) councillors in 2014 and an increase to 14 in 2016. UKIP takes a very traditional view of British history. Their Deputy Leader, Peter Whittle, has outlined 'fifty reasons to be proud of Britain', which include William Shakespeare, the King James Bible, Sir Isaac Newton, Peter Pan, the abolition of the slave trade and Winston Churchill. He includes the Industrial Revolution: 'the transformation wrought by the mechanisation of all aspects of manufacturing and agriculture essentially ushered in the modern age. What began in Britain, as a result of British ingenuity, inventiveness and enterprise, eventually spread throughout the rest of the globe, changing the way life was lived forever' (Dixon, n.d.).

Looking back to the past in Rotherham combines easily with a sense of loss of identity alongside a loss of industry. So, during the 2016 EU referendum campaign, the *Guardian* reported: 'A retired builder [in Rotherham], who did not want to give his name, says the good jobs in coal and steel have been replaced by low-wage ones that eastern Europeans have taken up' (Helm, 2016).

In the EU referendum, more than two thirds of those who voted in Rotherham voted 'leave'. Many commentators considered that in the northern post-industrial towns, this was largely a vote against immigration and immigrants – including second, third and fourth generations.[1] The belief that migration has made a positive contribution to British history was rejected by enormous numbers. Britain's long history of ethnic diversity, which stretches back hundreds of years, was negated (see Visram, 2002; Fryer, 2010). The effect is that, as Paul Gilroy has argued:

> 'race' is pushed outside of history and into the realm of natural, inevitable events. This capacity to evacuate any historical dimension to black life remains a fundamental achievement of racist ideologies in this country … Racism rests on the ability to contain blacks in the present, to repress and to deny the past. (Gilroy, 1987, pp.11-12)

This exclusion is reproduced at local level, evicting minority ethnic communities from ownership of the past, preventing the establishment of roots in towns and cities, except as newcomers, being forever 'immigrants', however many generations separate arrival of their forebears. This then feeds into 'local history'. Malcolm Dick has shown how ethnic diversity in Birmingham has been narrated in many older local histories. He points to the city's history of ethnic minorities dating back to the 18th century, with Jewish, Irish, Italian people in the city and a small Black presence before 1914, followed by the arrival of Yemenis in the 1930s and then African-Caribbean and South Asians after 1945. Yet a history of the city written in the 1970s identified immigrants as a problem:

> Coloured people formed only a minority of the total of immigrants into Birmingham in the years 1939-70. They were, however, the most noticeable, and in some ways created more problems than white immigrants from other parts of the British Isles and from abroad. Not only were they marked out by the colour of their skin, but frequently, too, by their language difficulties. (Quoted in Dick, 2011, p.93)

George and Yanina Sheeran have highlighted how local historians have championed 'history from below' and that this encouraged a sense of the democratic and inclusive history that embraces working-class stories. But the Sheerans argue that:

> times have changed greatly and what is basically a postwar conception of inclusiveness no longer holds good. Far from being inclusive, much traditional local history seems unintentionally to have become relatively exclusive: its practitioners and students are largely ageing white adults, who pursue a curriculum that is almost wholly Anglo-centric as a result. (Sheeran and Sheeran, 2009, p.318)

David Killingray has argued that this exclusiveness has been reciprocated by a lack of engagement by minority ethnic communities in 'local history':

> although local history is a popular subject it seems not to be recognised by members of immigrant communities themselves, especially those from Asia, Africa, and the Caribbean, who regard it as not 'their' history. This does not mean, however, that they are not interested in their own communal local history, a local history from within. Their life experience has often been very different from that of members of the white host community: it is about being uprooted, travelling overseas, settling in a new land, interacting with a new culture, facing rebuffs and hostility from people of a different colour. (Killingray, 2011, p.8)

Histories of Rotherham

In this next section of the chapter we explore, in brief, some responses to issues of history and heritage in Rotherham. There have been a series of heritage projects undertaken by people from minority ethnic communities in the town, which have the potential to add significantly to a local history narrative. (Many of these projects are analysed in Pahl, 2014.) There is a clear understanding of this contribution and the way in which this empowers residents of Rotherham, creating a sense of pride that runs counter to the stigma attached to the town.

But despite projects on histories of migration, the 'official' record of the migrant and black and minority ethnic presence is sparse. The Clifton Park Museum barely reflects the experience of the town's minority ethnic residents, and the archives service for RMBC contains extremely limited collections on the ethnically diverse nature of Rotherham's population. Rotherham Heritage Services made some efforts to engage with the numerous local history and heritage services in the early 2000s, but sadly some of its more innovative projects, such as the Rotherham Show and Cultural Diversity Festivals, have not survived in digital form, rendering them largely invisible.

There are a variety of community activists working to ensure that the contribution of minority ethnic groups to the town's history are recognised and visible. Mariam Shah (2016), who is a community activist and participant in our writing workshops, considers that things have changed considerably in recent years, caused by declining industry and world events. She suggests that: 'Previously, Asian people were seen as hard-working because they had a corner shop or businesses. Now all you ever see is all the bad stuff. Times have changed so much.' In her experience, the 9/11 attacks in the United States in 2001 prompted a moment of historical change whose impact was felt in local circumstances. 'Rotherham has changed so much that people can't really understand it,' Mariam notes (Shah, 2016). She recounted how, after 9/11, the position of Muslims was questioned in the town, in myriad ways. As well as her personal response of wearing a headscarf, she organised heritage projects with young Muslim men, exploring the experience of their fathers and grandfathers in the steel industry in Rotherham.

Mariam Shah worked with Al–Muneera, a community group that organised activities for children from mostly Pakistani backgrounds, to teach them about their history and heritage. Their project, 'Sheffield City of Steel: Asian men's contribution', looked at their fathers' generation working in the steel industry. The project explored all aspects of migration and working in the steel industry in Rotherham and Sheffield. One interviewee, Mr Syed Kala Shah, recounted how he was injured at work. He lived in England for 56 years, until his death in the year of the project (2011). Mr Shah explained that he had served in the Indian army and left what would become Pakistan at the end of the 'German war'. He worked at Rotherham Forge, describing how:

> [w]e made rods, steel bars and strips … They even made materials for the Mangla Dam. Each bar was as thick as my leg and it was very long about 10 or 12 feet. We put them in the furnace and it got really hot and we would take it out and put it in the rolling mills … Once someone passed a bar to me but it was put on wrong. It got twisted and came

off and hit my arm. It was red hot, extremely hot. … I put my hand forward to protect me and moved with it. When the bar stopped moving and fell to the floor, I fell too. The others picked me up and when I looked at my arm, it was all burned. (Al-Muneera, 2011, p.21)

Such oral testimony reveals a globalised history, embedded locally, with men's arrival from Pakistan and their interest in the construction of a Pakistani dam in the 1960s. Mariam's project linked such migrant stories and industrial stories, and she saw the impact on the young men:

They actually valued being here more, if that makes sense. Before they had talked about identity and about how they were English but also Asian and the fact that they were Muslim as well and there was no real sense of belonging, whereas they could actually say now that my history is that my dad came and worked in the steel industry, it was a thriving industry and they worked for years and years and they were part of that, and the things that they made – because we took them on a tour to Magna [a museum of steel in Rotherham] and showed them that side of things. It was quite empowering to see. It had a positive impact on those boys and they appreciated them and valued them more and the elderly men felt really pleased with themselves because somebody was actually listening to what they had to say. (Shah, 2016)

Mariam utilises her knowledge of history to challenge the idea that industrial decline and immigration were co-dependent, and counters that migration contributed to industrial sustainability but that subsequently decline changed the atmosphere in the town:

If you look at Britain in the sixties, it was industrious, there was a lot of work for everybody and everybody just got on, whereas now there are fewer jobs and it's causing a lot of friction between communities because it's seen as though 'they are taking our jobs'. You can sometimes challenge that by going back to history … . Because I know about history, I can challenge things. (Shah, 2016)

Zanib Rasool (2016), another participant in the writing workshops, has led a variety of community and heritage projects. She also looks to the past: 'Rotherham has had a lovely past, with welcoming communities' (Rasool, 2016). Zanib worked on the 'Sheffield City of Steel' project, and saw it as a tribute to her own father, who was employed in the industry. Talking to Zanib, it was possible to *feel* one of the book's opening statements: 'Most importantly, their stories inspire us with their hopes, struggles and determination' (Al-Muneera, 2011, p.3). Again, for her, it was an assertion of the role of Pakistani immigrants in Britain's industrial achievement.

This demand for historical recognition at a local level underpins broader calls for recognition of ethnic minorities within the national story. It is not enough for black and Asian people to be considered national citizens. They need to be seen as contributing to identities of place, to have their histories recorded as being embedded in the towns and cities in which they live, and for their feelings about living in Britain to be recorded. An example is provided by Mrs R Begum, one of the interviewees for a Rotherham-based Heritage Lottery Fund project called 'Their lives, our history.' Mrs Begum came to the UK in 1974. She explained how she learned English and how this empowered her to travel across England:

> A lady used to come to my house to teach me English. She helped me with phrases and the alphabet. By the end of it, I could read the name of places and I even managed to catch the coach to Birmingham to visit my cousin, it was a great feeling of independence. Although I couldn't speak English very well I understood most of it. (Al-Muneera, 2007, p.22)

Such interviews position the lives of Pakistani women in England from within, revealing a growing confidence – her 'great feeling of independence' – and its impact on her choices. It is fitting that Mrs Begum travelled to Birmingham. The Library of Birmingham has developed an archive of migration, black, Asian and minority ethnic archives there called 'Connecting histories – Voices past and present,' which seeks to:

> share information about present work, activities and possibilities; and to think ahead towards the kinds of activities we would like to see in the city and how we want to see the city develop as a place to live, to work and seek inspiration in, through its heritage and history, and by sharing and increasing our knowledge about the city

and the groups and localities that comprise it. (Library of Birmingham, 2014)

A key part of the first phase of 'Connecting histories' in 2005-07 was gathering and cataloguing archive collections that reflected the city's diversity,[2] and an outcome can be seen in the special edition of the journal *Midland History* on 'Ethnic community histories in the Midlands' in 2011 (Dick and Dudrah, 2011). Such developments provide a model for other towns and cities like Rotherham.

The absence of the black and minority ethnic experience in the official record of Rotherham leads some to consider that a clean slate is needed. Zahir Rafiq (2016, see also Chapter Eighteen), a British Muslim artist, suggests that 'the establishment, the people who do this type of research ... tend to focus too much on history ... as a starting point'. Instead, he expresses his desire to establish a new base point from which subsequent history could be made, written or, in his case, painted through portraits of British Muslims as Rotherham residents, capturing the variety of ways in which Muslims engage with culture and leisure. Rather than starting with the past, Zahir focuses on capturing the present, with a mind towards creating future histories (Rafiq, 2016): 'I feel that the artwork takes a life of its own. They become artefacts. They become part of history. They become used as what the Muslim community at this point in time were like.'

Due to the scale of decline in the coal and steel industries at the end of the 20th century, Rotherham, like many other post-industrial towns and cities, faces a crisis of identity, in which landscapes have been devastated and communities have been stigmatised, bringing loss of hope and loss of pride. (For transnational comparisons, see Mah, 2012.) The resulting local history narrative often links deindustrialisation and subsequent poverty with post-war immigration. We have called this connection between immigration and urban decay a 'local history paradigm', in which positive features of the past are privileged, and history is seen as coming to an end in the 1980s. The view that there has been further decline of both morals and urban decay as a result of immigration has deepened in the 21st century, as crimes of child sexual exploitation, committed by men mainly of Pakistani Muslim heritage, have become associated with Rotherham.

Local histories of Rotherham, printed and digital, have adhered to this paradigm, romanticising the distant and industrial pasts and conveying a sense of loss. The result has been the exclusion of immigrant and ethnic minority communities from local history. However, recent heritage projects undertaken by people from minority ethnic communities, have tried to take some ownership of the past and to present stories that challenge the 'local history paradigm', by having their contributions to the town's history recognised. Community activists draw on personal experiences and use history to counter traditional dialogues, in order to move local history beyond the 1980s 'endpoint'. Others aim to create a new starting point for history, by documenting the present.

Despite many people in minority ethnic communities engaging in projects to add to the local history narrative and to create artefacts of the present, their histories have not always become a part of the mainstream discourse. They have been largely absent from the archives and libraries. The need for such historical or heritage activism, to ensure that minority ethnic communities are represented in archives, university courses, cultural institutions and popular discourse, underscores the importance of the co-production of historical knowledge. This does not just apply in the local context of Rotherham or the north of England, but is of global concern. The question of who 'owns' history – and how historical narratives are reproduced and represented – emerges continually in a variety of geographical and historical contexts to show questions of power in history. The 'history wars' in Australia are paralleled by opposition to indigenous historical narratives and methodologies across the world, in which histories outside the mainstream are denied and erased (see, for example, Clark, 2013).

Academic historians *alone* are certainly not best situated to enable or advocate new forms of history that challenge power and knowledge structures for, as Kuokkanen (2008) argues: 'the academy is based fundamentally on a very narrow understanding of the world' (p.2). This book is a small step in moving the history of Rotherham beyond the local history paradigm to a narrative that is more diverse and inclusive in acknowledging the contributions of minority ethnic communities to making and writing Rotherham's local and global history.

Notes

[1] Of course, the Brexit vote was more complex than being solely anti-immigration. Nationally, about one third of South Asian Britons voted to leave the EU. See www.politico.eu/article/immigrants-who-voted-for-brexit-luton-migration/.

[2] www.connectinghistories.org.uk.

SEVEN

Silk and steel

Shahin Shah

The pictures in this chapter were produced by Shahin Shah. They were commissioned in response to the 'Imagine' project's focus on the histories and cultures of Rotherham, particularly around the themes of 'silk and steel'. They offer a historical account of what it was like to come to the UK, but they also depict: a felt and embodied response to the hardships and loneliness of a young bride coming to the UK; the experience of a British Asian man working in the steel mills; a suitcase filled with special memories; and the visceral experience of racism for a young child. Taken together, these images are living history. Shahin Shah describes them here in the context of her life in Rotherham.

The bride

This image (Figure 7.1) narrates the journey of my mother coming to this country and the loneliness she and others, some of whom were child brides, endured. The picture is divided in two, reflecting different emotional and lived experiences of women at that time, the migrant experience of loss of home and place.

The colour represents the vibrant sunshine and light they left behind, the freedom of the rural land, the familiar informality of friends and family to come to our new home: a cold, dismal place, where it snowed or rained a lot, the unfamiliar industrial fumes, the darkened sky. Being stuck in a two–up, two–down terraced house all day brought on a feeling never before known to many, of claustrophobia often teamed with the isolation of not knowing anyone. Any communication now was of a formal nature, with a doctor, a midwife, a teacher, along with the language and culture, which were both a mystery.

Due to the almost forced transition, as many women did not have a say in becoming a migrant, women yearned for their homeland, and held on dearly to their now even more treasured memories. This is depicted not just in the physical journey from the colour rainbow of

53

vibrant life cultures and the finding of coal instead of gold at the end of the rainbow, but also signals the emotional attachment many women had with their homeland and the significance of their memories. These memories were the emotional bridge to the home they left behind.

Figure 7.1: The bride

The steel man

Steel: hard, cold and robust like the burning embers of the steel factories. Men such as my father worked long hours, doing jobs that no one else wanted to. Figure 7.2 captures the sweat and toil of working in a steel factory for years until old age.

The final journey, when work is done, for many men is the ultimate journey, the one they saved up their entire lives for – to travel to the pilgrimage to Mecca, the Hajj. That is what they worked for all those years without rest or negligence of duty, to live a humble life, to work all the God-given hours, to provide for their families without complaint of the uncompassionate world of hard labour. The liquid gold that turned hard and cold. They did not have the education and knowledge of the physics associated with the metals, but had the experience of having their hands burnt by it. They knew that better than anyone else. Dutifully they earned their living, raised their children and then finally, after a lifetime of saving, embarked upon the pilgrimage to seek solace and salvation in prayer in the place where everybody of every colour, of every culture, of every social disposition was accepted.

Figure 7.2: The steel man

The suitcase

A migrant and their suitcase. It was never just a container of things, it was the *palanquin* (carrier) of memories and for memories. Wherever the suitcase went, the memories went too (see Figure 7.3).

Truly, 'the suitcase' was indeed a treasure trove to remember home. Each object holds a memory dear and that loss of home. Everyone's suitcase is unique to their own individual story, the journey they travelled. Kept in there are letters from home that our parents read and read again from their family, when yearning for home was too great. These objects became artefacts, reminding them of who they once were, held with love, care and respect. Tears dissolved some of the words on the aged paper, but the messages were etched in their hearts forever. Sometimes when the children were asleep, the suitcase was opened, but nothing was taken out. For those who knew their homeland found the scent of home packed inside it.

Every household had a suitcase. It had its prized place, on top of the wardrobe, under the bed, beside the chest of drawers. It was 'the suitcase' and everyone in the household knew which one.

Figure 7.3: The suitcase

Racism

Racism. That word. Real racism. It always rears its ugly head and those people who experience unkind and unforgiven words cannot forget them. The words are left unforgiven not because they are unforgivable, but because forgiveness has never been sought for either word or action. So the racism is left unforgiven.

This image (see Figure 7.4) tries to articulate the fear resulting from racist attacks and how they manifest in many different forms – it may be words, actions, the instigation of animals, or isolation.

Can a dog be racist? A peculiar question, but the image depicts children running in all directions, trying to get home, desperately trying to get away from the dog set on them by a racist. I remember that experience as if it were today, not yesterday. That's how profoundly dangerous and fearful it felt. The inability of the authorities to keep the racists at arm's length is shown, with the obvious blunder evident in the image of the safety barricade of men and might being stationed in the wrong place, leaving racists free to verbally, physically and emotionally scar and set their dogs on us. The chaos depicted in the image and experienced by the victims shows that it is harder to tame a racist than a dog. That racism still hits me today.

Figure 7.4: Racism

Challenging racism through art

An artist's own experience is central to the artwork. The artist also situates herself in the experience of others in order to understand those emotions that people fear; the fear and pain are invested in the drawing and paintings, reliving the memory with every stroke. Threading stories through art, the artist is able to speak of a thousand untold words, which transcend cultural and language barriers. An image can stay in the mind of the audience long after the words have disappeared. Sticks and stones might break my bones, but the image will forever haunt me.

Being subjected to racism at first hand and being an Asian artist, I have illustrated the distraught happenings that became regular occurrences of my childhood days. As a child, my only form of self-defence was to save small stones in my pockets, which gave me a little time to 'run' in the event of racist attacks by the skinheads and National Front.

South Asian artists, like myself and Zahir Rafiq (see Chapter Eighteen), are best placed to tell stories of our heritage. We heard those stories at first hand and we experienced the emotions that came with them. Indigenous English artists, no matter how well meaning, cannot 'get it' right. There has to be an emotional link to those stories – those stories are reminders of our heritage, as we negotiate new roots in other parts of the world.

Sadly, history is repeating itself and racism is taking different forms. As a society, we have not been able to change it. However, using art – and through arts practice – everyone can challenge racism, and perhaps bring it to an end.

EIGHT

History and co-production in the home: documents, artefacts and migrant identities in Rotherham

William Gould and Mariam Shah

Britain's island story has traditionally been a narrative of industry, progress, liberalism at home and overseas, and the developing politics of race relations and experiments in progressive self-government around the world. Recent celebrations of Magna Carta, for example, as the benevolent root of constitutions globally, illustrate this long-term trend.

Behind this narrative lie public notions of British history that still cling to the importance of the Second World War. Recently, this has led to the decision to place the image of Winston Churchill on the reverse of the £5 note. Victory in 1945 is celebrated as Britain's 'finest hour' – either as a moment of national celebration or as a period in the growth of the welfare state. It is rarely viewed as a defining moment for British decolonisation, the effects of which both directly affected urban communities across Britain and indirectly produced modes of democratic co-existence, citizenship and social tolerance. Still less, have the public in general been invited to engage with the violence of colonialism itself, and the outcomes of the long-term conflicts it generated for contemporary global crises. The major histories of the isles instead treat the presence of South Asians, for example, as Commonwealth movement of peoples providing labour for mid-century regeneration – sojourners forging ethnic enclaves in the hearts of Britain's industrial centres. The voices of these 'ethnic minorities' are mediated by majorities and by the state.

This marginalisation of alternative public historical narratives for Britain has had its impact on the perception of those regions transformed by Commonwealth migration from the middle of the 20th century and, in particular, the large industrial cities of the Midlands and the North. Perpetuating the myth of 'grim up north', relative under-investment, an erosion of cultural institutions in favour of the South East, has been part of this trend. This process has also created the idea of Bradford as a 'failed' multicultural experiment, and contributed to the branding of Rotherham as a problem city. For the Yorkshire and Humber region, Leeds, Sheffield, Rotherham and Bradford make up around 36% of the region's total population. These four cities have disproportionately large South Asian populations – nearly 70% for the region. In this sense, the contemporary demographic history of the UK's large northern cities is marked by postcolonial migration alongside industrial decline.

There were significant South Asian populations in the UK well in advance of the post-war period (Visram, 2002), but structures of British Asian neighbourhoods in these cities formed from the 1950s to 1960s. Of a total population of 260,100 in 2015, the South Asian population of Rotherham was 8,600 (with the vast majority, around 7,900, originating from Pakistan or Kashmir), constituting nearly 40% of the city's total Black and minority ethnic population. The majority of these residents (77%) are concentrated in three of the city's 21 wards – Rotherham West, Rotherham East and Boston Castle, with a focus on the regions of Eastwood, Ferham, Masbrough, Wellgate and Broom Valley, but with more recent movement into the areas of Broom and Moorgate.[1] This spatial clustering is a feature of many other cities in the UK and in particular in places such as Birmingham (Gale, 2014, pp.118-20).

In many UK cities, especially those of the industrial Midlands and the North, where such urban concentrations are pronounced, a sense of national belonging has for long been articulated in relation to the idea of the city on the one hand and the role of the family on the other. This has meant that the notion of a 'British Asian' or 'British Muslim' identity has been closely tied to a civic consciousness, often relating different cities with each other across each region (McLoughlin, 2014, p.4). Key to this sense of national belonging are historical memories, in which histories of labour are linked to a sense of the international role of family networks, or nodes within a cultural and political economy (Kaur and Kalra, 1996, p.229).

This civic identity relates partly to histories of migration, their controls and perceptions of institutional racism. Migration to 'beat the ban' of the Immigration Act 1962 and the Commonwealth Immigration Act 1968 vouchers[2] marked northern and Midlands cities (12,823 Indians and Pakistanis entered the UK in January and February 1968). The attractiveness of these cities, however, went beyond the conveniences of chain migration. By the 1970s, for example, some Bradfordians had adopted the colloquial 'Bradistan' and, as we will see later in this chapter, in many towns across the North, specific community organisations have been rooted in a sense of place and belonging. South Asian migration to the UK, then, was not just a response to a post-war labour shortage, but was also driven by multiple forms of network building across cities and continents.

In order to understand these alternative histories of urban settlement, we need to look at the intersection between family and neighbourhood. The difficulty for historians and others exploring this process is in many respects methodological. So far, the approaches of historians in this area has been defined broadly under the term 'social history'– a field that has been most sensitive to ethnicity, gender, education, labour and family. Despite moving away from a study of 'social structures' from the 1980s (Lloyd, 1991), the discipline has struggled with the methodological task of writing histories 'from the bottom up' or for and by the social subjects of enquiry (Magnusson, 2003). Instead, there has been a call away from metanarratives, towards a consideration of 'singular' cultural reference points, and the need to separate historical 'traces' from their representation by the historian as 'historical knowledge' (Munslow, 1997). This chapter proposes a form of co-production that connects specific small-scale communities not to meta-histories, but to documents that have a specific meaning within their own notions of narrative. The 'stuff' of such histories, because they are as much about the private, intimate and familiar, is about stuff in the home – much of it undiscovered, perhaps only half-realised by families. Many historians have seen this as the ephemera of marginal oral histories. In extension of arguments about the role of oral history made elsewhere (Gould and Qureshi, 2014), we argue that the connection between the intimate, which includes the material memorabilia and personal documents in homes, and the public community, helps us to explore the ways in which ideas of postcolonial citizenship are related to the idea of the home.

We might think of this as an interaction between alternative registers of writing, permitting a view of how private and public stories are mediated through a relationship between official documentation on the one hand and oral recollections on the other. In other words, we are interested in the relationship between formal, paper texts and oral traditions. This is not new to the discipline of history and certainly not to anthropology. In the latter field, Vazira Jacoobali Zamindar, for example, examined experiences of India's partition, in relation to official notions of movement and documents allowing communities to move or migrate (or restricting their movement) and life/family histories (Zamindar, 2007). Emma Tarlo looked at the period of India's Emergency in the 1970s, to explore the relationship between sterilisation certificates and stories of people who were subject to state surveillance and slum clearance (Tarlo, 2003). For both of these authors, there was an interesting dichotomy between paper and everyday truths – something that we were keen to explore in relation to family histories, particularly those of migration, intergenerational tales and notions of public identity.

Life cycles of the family

We worked with three Rotherham families from varying backgrounds – two originating from Pakistan and a third from Yemen. For all three, this experience of the relationship between material and written oral history contrasted in important ways. But in all cases, family memorabilia and objects served the purpose of fixing narratives about such events as rites of passage, intergenerational relationships and, perhaps most crucially, links between the home/family or city and homes overseas.

The main representative and interviewee of our first family, Mrs M. Shah, is a 40-year-old British Pakistani with strong family networks in Rotherham. She does extensive work in the local community, particularly for women's groups, and is the first female Muslim Chaplain in Rotherham. The representative of our second family was Mr Mukhtar Ahmed, who arrived in the UK in 1961, from Gujjar Khan, Pakistan. At a young age, he had worked on the Pakistan railways, and in Rotherham he worked in the W. N. Baines Valve Factory. Nasser Ali was the interview for our third family. Originating in Yemen from a farming community and aged 75 at the time of our interview in 2016, he came to the UK in 1970, first to Sheffield for six years and then to work in Rotherham Forge and for Firth Brown.

In the two families of Pakistani origin, a number of patterns became clear.

- First, there was a strong reliance on an oral and emotional archive: the birth of children, house moves and so on, were remembered or recounted more clearly than the career changes and events of elders. In the case of the Shah family, this involved the initially obscured account of the elder Mr Shah's role in military service. Official 'dates' were usually recorded strongly in relation to the life cycle of the family, rather than in relation to political or contextual changes. But this happened more commonly in relation to bureaucratic or contextual necessity, such as passports and schooling.
- Second, the very process of recovering stories about the families created a new historical awareness, in which new kinds of questions were asked within the family itself. Sometimes, at mundane levels,

this led to some surprising miscommunications about the lives of family members.

When we interviewed the elder Mrs Shah, she talked about her childhood without any reference to dates. She knew that she was a child bride, as was common at the time, and that her husband was considerably older, but did not know her wedding date or husband's date of birth. Her husband was an orphan, so nobody could confirm when he was born, leading to it being recorded as 1 January. This was quite common among first-generation migrant communities. Similarly, the elder Mrs Shah was not sure of her own year of birth, because her age had been exaggerated on her passport application. However, the dates of birth of each of her nine children, even those she had lost, tripped off her tongue effortlessly, perhaps because most were British born, and even those that were not needed passports. We wondered whether life in Britain had perhaps given the elder Mrs Shah a better understanding of the importance of recording these events for official documentation. She had even remembered all her Rotherham addresses over the last 40 years. The theme of family miscommunication was most clearly illustrated in the scars on the back of Mr Shah's shoulder, which the main family interviewee had always assumed were war wounds. The respondent's mother, by contrast, maintained that they were in fact scars from smallpox.

Mr Mukhtar Ahmed's story was one of a lone male migrant, who sought work in the UK so as to remit wages back to Pakistan. Here too, the oral testimony connected narratives of emotional importance to specific local events. He talked about the sense of how each man labouring in the steelworks referred to family 'back home'. 'We didn't just have ourselves to think about', he suggested, but mixed in with the sense of duty to support family back home, were also feelings of longing – eating roti together, seeing family and friends on special occasions. 'Going back' would have been a sign of failure. Equally, the difficulties of life in the UK, work–home balance, were a means of reflecting on the idea of home in different places, as we will see later. The 'events' of the family were mixed up with dates of new significance in the UK – the birth of Mr Mukhtar Ahmed's brother in Pakistan was related to the setting up of the first Rotherham mosque in 1957. Whereas the latter was something everyone in the community talked about, Mr Mukhtar Ahmed didn't hear about the birth of his brother until two years later, due to postal delays. Slowly, Mr Mukhtar Ahmed's family members joined him in Rotherham.

Mr Nasser Ali was also a sole male migrant, whose family joined him 15 years after his first arrival in the UK. Moving between jobs on the recommendations and with the help of friends, he spent six years in Sheffield before moving to Rotherham, working variously as a 'hook man' on a crane, in a scissor factory and for Royal Mail. Mr Ali also stressed the importance of helping family 'back home' as foundational to his identity and sense of belonging to the city and the country. In other words, he talked about the plight of family back in Yemen in the context of hard work undertaken in the UK. The sense of duty and identity, both in domestic and public contexts, was reinforced via this transfer of material wealth and help, for kin who were unable to find the same kind of employment as him. The idea of belonging, both internally and from the point of view of majority UK communities, was established by the knowledge of hard work and its importance to family life in other contexts.

Family objects and daily life

It was clear that for all of the families there was then a relationship between the public sense of identity and belonging and particular 'domestic' circumstances and events. In the case of Mr Mukhtar Ahmed, this was best illustrated in the everyday events and routines of life in the UK, as a person separated from larger family networks. The routines surrounding meals back home were imagined as a distant memory, but kept the family rooted, despite separation. At the same time, they justified the work:

> We all worked so hard, we had too many reasons to. It was what kept us going. Some days we didn't even have time to eat – what we took for breakfast would often serve as our evening meal. Back home we would be treated with delicious meals lovingly cooked by our mothers and sisters – and here if you didn't learn how to cook you would soon go hungry!

For Mr Mukhtar Ahmed, this was also an occasion to reflect on the differential ideas of 'sacrifice' that the older or first generations had made for the second and third generations.

Nasser Ali was also keen to relate the routines of life to his very reasons for staying on and his sense of identification with the UK. He discussed how, in the early years, he was forced to work 'week to week', but that it was still nevertheless possible to save enough to support his family back home. It was clear that this struggle, however, led him to view those early years in a positive light. When we asked him whether he had any family mementos or documents from those times in the UK, he described, with pride, the number of different passports he had held – 10 in total. For Mr Nasser Ali, this was an indication of his rootedness and commitment to the UK. But there had been no reason to hold onto the past – most of his older documents had been lost. In contrast, when Nasser Ali's wife joined the interview, it was clear that Mr Nasser Ali's view of the past was constructed as a largely beneficial struggle against adversity: there were many aspects to his life in the UK that had not been altogether positive.

After enquiring about the possible possessions of the elder Mr Shah from our first family, there was discussion of a 'box of belongings' stored in the house that the family had rarely disturbed. The item was known to exist in the house, and to contain something of the past, including 'some medals and other documents'. The contents were known but their significance was not explored, and it was agreed that there were many things about Mr Shah that the family were only dimly aware of. In this box we found some medals. There was no particular sense that they were something to treasure and there had been no retelling of a legendary story of Mr Shah's bravery. The family did not know how he had acquired the medals, what they represented, or that they were medals from the British Indian army. Following further research, we discovered that the medals were awarded for 'general service'. We discussed the image of the King Emperor on the back, and the notion of solidarity with 'Empire'. This was a novel idea, but the family did discuss them as a source of family honour and they clearly meant different things to different generations. Mr Shah had travelled the world with the army – a sign to the family that he was cosmopolitan.

A second document held in Mr Shah's box was his old passport. This contained the usual photo page, with name, date of birth and distinguishing marks. It also had a large number of entry and exit stamps. Sitting with the family, we looked at the text and talked about the tensions it contained: 'To allow the bearer to pass freely without let or hindrance, and to afford assistance and protection of which he may stand in need.'

On the one hand, this suggested promises of movement and freedoms. On the other, it also signified restrictions on those freedoms, or forms of surveillance, via bodily identity markers: the document marked and categorised its holder. Both the text and its subtexts, on further discussion, took on significance within the family's history, especially as Mr Shah had brought the document as an initial migrant from South Asia. In particular, we discussed how the passport brought certain freedoms, but at the cost of situating and limiting identity and forms of citizenship. These physical descriptions stood as a memory of this father figure for later generations.

The passport illustrated two other things: the multi-local nature of the family's history and how that history related to timings of movements and returns; and the building of a sense of cosmopolitanism, which surpassed a strict sense of belonging to the town itself. Mr Shah was celebrated by his family as someone who had travelled widely, and his identity was mixed up with that travel. His past also related to, and was bound up with, global struggle or war.

Finally, we explored the ways in which the markings of identity on the passport – their links to official and unofficial dates – related, firstly, to an official record and secondly to the particularities of the family and its movement between different spaces. We were interested in how far these dates corresponded to narrated family histories and, in a sense, what lay behind them unofficially.

There was also a link between these documents and other, contemporary objects in the home, which often seamlessly featured in our conversations. Principal here was our discussion of Mrs M. Shah's hijab and what it meant to wear this in relation to national and international events. Mrs M. Shah recounted how there was a direct relationship between, for example, a sense of 'reaction' to Muslims in the town following 9/11 and her decision to wear the hijab. We discussed how the act of wearing was as much about community and family within the context of Rotherham, as about Islam. Importantly, Mrs M. Shah noted that the significance of this object was its many positional meanings. Some, she felt, had portrayed the hijab as being in 'opposition' to British values. She herself considered it to be an instrument of power and liberation within British society. It allowed her to participate in public spaces more freely than before, since it made her identity boundaries clearer to everyone without having to articulate it. For example, previously, she felt that she had to be one person at work and another at home. In this sense, the hijab integrated private and public identities. Finally, it brought a sense of personal clarity – being unsure, for a while, about her place within the community, the hijab marked a very specific Muslim identity, rather than one that was necessarily hybrid or compromised by specific spaces.

Objects, place and process: some conclusions

The three families we interviewed in Rotherham were keen to engage with their own personal histories, and were quite clear about how they were characterised by long-term struggles in making a living, as divided families across different continents. For all our participants, more important than the wider context of the town and especially national politics was the interweaving of the public lives of work and migration, with the intimate and domestic realities of the home, and its material consequences. For each interviewee, questions of identity, translocality (living simultaneously in different spaces and places), freedom and restriction were mediated through different registers, moving between home and transnational living.

This is not to argue that such oral histories are somehow just particular accounts of the first- or second-generation Pakistani community experiences. Within these personal and familial histories private artefacts, of historical importance to the family, take on a public significance. The effect of these documents on personal histories is nuanced and changeable. Certain public texts and pieces of writing have a great significance in a particular moment but fade into the background later, and become virtually invisible – like memory itself. One question we asked ourselves as researchers was: at what point, then, do the monumental texts become 'everyday' – and what is the significance of these things being part of our everyday environment? In the case of all three interviewees, these documents, artefacts or texts were domesticated or 'put away' in the home. They became a part of a family's half-remembered background about each of its members. But they reappeared at points at which families decided (either prompted or not) to revisit their history.

More important, then, than these reflections on the materials of the home, has been the process of the research itself for everyone. For our participants, discussing the history of family objects has ignited a new form of historical curiosity. This may seem mundane. However, its effects are potentially huge, both within families and across communities, since it opens up new connections in the minds of participants between the domestic and public aspects of their lives, and how they are both mediated by different forms of historical memory.

For the interviewers, interaction and collaboration has forced us to think in new ways about the texts and forms of writing we see in public or private spaces. Perhaps most importantly, it requires all co-producers never to take for granted the ways in which historical narratives are mediated, and consider how that mediation itself helps to reform memories and reconnect them to objects in the home.

Notes

1 Rotherham Demographic Profile 2015, *Rotherham Joint Strategic Needs Assessment*, pp. 9-11, http://www.rotherham.gov.uk/jsna/download/downloads/id/99/rotherham_demographic_profile_2015.pdf.

2 In 1968 the UK government introduced controls in the Commonwealth Immigration Act of that year, by requiring all Commonwealth citizens with no connection 'by birth or descent' to Britain, to obtain an entry voucher before arriving. A certain quota of vouchers was allowed per year (at first 150); the policy was a clear attempt to limit non-white immigration to the UK. See James Patrick Lynch and Rita James Simon (2003), *Immigration the World Over: Statutes, Policies and Practices*, Lanham MD: Rowman and Littlefield, p. 125.

NINE

Tassibee: a case study

Khalida Luqman

Tassibee is a locally respected charity, originally founded in 1993 as a volunteer-led support group for isolated and socially excluded Pakistani women in Rotherham. Over the years, the centre has delivered a range of successful, innovative and capacity-building projects that focus on transforming the lives of British Muslim Asian women, by creating opportunities for women of all ages. Tassibee encourages improved health and wellbeing, using the social model of understanding and alleviating loneliness; this encourages different generations of women, such as young and elderly women, single mothers, widows and carers, to come together. The organisation won Project of the Year at Rotherham Community Achievement Awards in 2015 for making an outstanding contribution to people and communities in the city for over 25 years.

The centre works with first-generation migrants, including recently married women, and older dependants who have come to this country to join other family members. Our long-standing relationships with many partner organisations, alongside our religious and cultural credibility in the community, enable us to do this successfully. Tassibee also recognises that there are children living in second- and third-generation households with parents speaking no English.

Here I present excerpts of writing and reflections by three participants who regularly attended the Tassibee programmes: Nasim Bashir, Fazelat Begum and Mukhtar Begum. They detail the previous lives of the first generation of women who came to the UK from Pakistan in the 1960s. These women's writing reflects memories of life prior to arriving in the UK, at which point everything changed for them. The different cultural lifestyle in the UK was not something that the women could ever have imagined. They found it hard to adapt to the British weather, especially snow, the language, not having seen white people before, and the concept of education for all children, including girls. They experienced difficulties with accessing services, including health and dental services, and social support in terms of provision (available only if you had the skills to access it). Even the houses were a cultural shock, as those in Pakistan are more open, and to bathe you had to either use a tin bath or find a public bathing place.

Reflections by three Tassibee participants

Nasim Bashir

I remember my first ever visit to the Tassibee project. It was a Friday prayer group, there were many women present, and they were all wearing white. I felt good and special to be with all the women. My previous feelings of isolation and loneliness appeared to have vanished and I felt special. I am not a very religious person but when I mixed with these women, I had an overwhelming feeling of belonging and desire to pray. The experience was a powerful one and one I remember vividly to this day.

I was born in the small town of Jhelum in Punjab, Pakistan, into an educated family and I was intellectual myself, very much interested in learning. We were all interested in Urdu literature.

I am well educated and was a respected woman in Pakistan, however, when I moved to England I was not able to develop my skills. Language, a common barrier amongst educated Pakistani women, and poor confidence meant I was not able to embrace my skills. Khalida recognised that I had skills that would be of benefit to Tassibee. I have a talent for writing, particularly speeches. Through Tassibee I have been able to utilise my skills that have increased my self-confidence and utilised skills that were otherwise dormant.

Fazelat Begum

I want to tell you about my childhood. I was born in Jhelum, Pakistan and I spent all my childhood there.

In those days, there were not any colourful toys for children. The land and houses were all made of mud, when we children played we used to make pots out of the mud and play with them. With old clothes, we used to make bride and groom dolls and then plan a wedding. On the wedding day, we used to dance and sing – just like the older generation. The girls used to make swings on trees and the boys used to play with marbles and kites. In the evening with a clear sky, sparkling stars and a full moon, we used to play hide and seek using the light from the moon, as there weren't any streetlights.

There were not many schools so education was considered more important for boys, although there was not as much pressure as nowadays. In the village, there was no electricity so for a bit of a breeze it was common to sleep outside under the trees and when the heat became unbearable people used hand fans.

In some households when there is a girl born, a family relative will come and tie a piece of thread on the girl and say 'I will have this girl as my daughter-in-law in the near future'.

I would like to tell you about my own marriage as an example. I never saw my husband before our marriage although I am very lucky, as he is a loving, kind and perfect man. I feel that love is only gained after marriage, but today it is believed that it is necessary to meet, talk and see each other before marriage. When I was young we respected our elders and accepted chastisement but nowadays the young ones can't accept this. The younger generation should understand that the relationship a husband and wife share is one where you should love and look after one another – to be able to live as one hereafter.

I came to England in 1961. I did not like anything when I came here, as it was so cold outside. The only option was to stay at home, even if I wanted to go out I could not speak the language, and I could not watch TV for the same reason.

In my house, there were no bathroom facilities indoors – we shared an outdoor toilet with a neighbour, each household having their own key, and sometimes there was a queue. At night, there was no light so we had to carry a torch. There was no central heating in the house so we used to light a coal fire.

In our country village, life was so simple and happy. There, waking up in the morning, listening to the birds, collecting milk and then preparing breakfast was such a pleasure – a treasured memory.

Mukhtar Begum

I was born in Rawal Pindi, which is a famous district of Pakistan. I went to a local school and completed my early primary education. I did GCSE at one of the local secondary schools.

My husband lived in a village but he left to go to Kohat for his training as he had joined the army. There is a huge difference between lifestyles in a city and small village. In the city, we had a better standard of life and more facilities, such as electricity, clean water, gas and sewage systems. In the city we lived in the main area, which had supermarkets and shopping centres, whereas in the village, it was a different story, initially everything seemed different and strange to me.

In 1991, we all came to England, as my husband was transferred to the High Commission of Pakistan in London. Later my son was married and settled in England while I returned to Pakistan, but I have now come back to England to see my son and his family.

I grew up in a city in Pakistan that was very busy and I was always on the go. It was important to me that I educate myself and so I qualified as a teacher in Pakistan. I am from a family of teachers, my sisters and aunties either taught or were principles at the local schools.

I continued to live in Pakistan with my family and husband. My children grew up and my eldest son moved to England. I was happy living in Pakistan and have fond memories. When my husband died, I was left feeling sad and lonely. I decided to move to England to be with my eldest son.

It was difficult for me to adjust to living in England. I felt lonely and bored in my son's house. My son and daughter-in-law worked during the day and my grandchildren were at school. I did not really know anybody and I did not feel confident using the transport services that could have increased my sense of independence. I felt isolated in the house and this was affecting my mental health. My son recognised I was feeling isolated and recommended I become involved with Tassibee. I met with Khalida and soon afterwards, I began attending some of the sessions and Tassibee events.

The women's writing is a window into the worlds of first-generation migrant women, who came from Pakistan to this sometimes cold, hard country. These reflections serve to give these women a voice in addressing the isolation they experienced. By sharing their stories with women from different generations, the process of reflection and writing becomes a tool for lessening loneliness and fostering improved wellbeing.

TEN

Identity

Zanib Rasool

In the UK, there is an increased focus on social cohesion and integration (Casey, 2016; DCLG).[1] Young people from minority ethnic communities experience a great deal of pressure in order to fit in with the national narrative of 'Britishness', and often feel that they should conform outwardly in their dress and physical appearance, and adopt British sociocultural practices. Those individuals who maintain their faith, language and cultural identity are seen as segregating themselves and living parallel lives (Miah, 2012). However, racial harassment can have a 'corrosive effect on [the] lives of minority ethnic households, impacting on attitudes and behaviour and restricting opportunities' (Cole and Robinson, 2003, p.22).

Young people from minority ethnic communities will spend a lifetime on self-exploration and negotiating their contested identities. Paul Ward argues, 'British identity has never been static or fixed but has fluctuated in meaning as different Britons have made claims upon it' (Ward, 2004, p.172). Identity is fluid and changeable over time and space.

I focus here on the identities of British Muslim young women who I worked with in a writing group, and share some of the themes that emerged during our writing sessions. Three specific themes related to identity came out of the girls' writing group: place and globalisation; religion; and language.

Identity, place and globalisation

When I was a teenager in the 1970s, my identity was strongly attached to my neighbourhood. The street where I resided was home to me and others from the same Pakistani cultural background as my parents. This allowed us to maintain the strong traditions from Pakistan of community networks and collective responsibility. The street where I lived as a child was also home to a few Irish, Italian and Polish families, who were immigrants like us. At the end of the street, there was the epitome of British culture, a pub, as well as a fish and chip shop and a corner store that sold everything from milk to shoelaces.

Christensen (2003) argues that children 'map personal biographies and engage with place as a simultaneously located and physical location, describing how they come to inhabit and belong to a place through their experiences and use of it' (Christensen and O'Brien, 2003, p.15). It was fun growing up on my street, as I remembered during the writing group sessions:

> A narrow grimy old street with terrace houses that which looked almost the same
> Mothers pushing their reluctant children outdoors so they can get their housework done and the washing out to dry whilst the weather was good
> Children played outside, hop-scotch, marbles and footy in the corner of the street, girls with their small brothers or sisters in pushchairs, pretending to be mummy's for the day
> We played in the street until it was almost dark when we were dragged inside by our mothers wanting us in bed so they could have some peace

In summer 2014, a group of women, all school friends of mine, recorded their memories of growing up in Rotherham as an oral history to capture what life was like for children of immigrants growing up in a northern town in the 1970s. The discussion often referred to the difference between today's young generation and how we grew up. One theme to emerge from our discussion was that of the close-knit community we experienced:

> We use[d] to go to each other's house and play a lot. We use[d] to go walking in the fields close by with an Auntie on our street.

> We use[d] to exchange curry dishes, my mum would make me take a dish down the street to your house and then you would come up the street with something your mum had cooked.

> Modern technology has taken over, the young generations want too much privacy, their friendship circle is wider, and ours was face-to-face contact.

> We use[d] to be out in the snow until 10'clock at night.

Another theme was the responsibilities we had around the home:

> We were more responsible, we were made to grow up. I was the eldest and became a mother figure to my younger siblings.

> Home from school, we would help with cooking, when we came home, I use[d] to cook chapatti with my brother.

> We did not have central heating; my younger brother would light the coal fire every day before he went to school.

> People had less money then, but were creative, valued each other and not things.

Entertainment was also a prominent theme:

> We use[d] to look forward to Saturdays because *Banana Split* was on tele, on this little black and white tele.

> I use[d] to love the Osmonds and use[d] to save my pennies to buy *Jackie*.[2]

> I remember the Bay City Rollers had at a teatime show, I use[d] to run home from school to watch rather than wait for the bus and get late.

My teenage years revolved around a small black and white television set, which had two channels, and a few teenage girls' magazines. Today, young people live in a multicultural, multidimensional and multimodal world. Kress (2010) refers to 'representational and communicational practices that are constantly altered and modified in line with social changes' (p.7). He talks of different modes of communication, including art forms (dance, music, images and videos), social semiotic resources (such as texting, Twitter, Facebook, Instagram and blogging) and semiotic resources (such as smartphones, iPads and laptops), which all connect today's young people to a much wider world then mine.

The conversations with my friends show how, when growing up, our identity was shaped primarily from a local perspective. Tuan (2001) suggests that space and place are basic components of the lived experience: 'place is security and space is freedom' (p.3). Place for the girls in the writing group was a home that provided them with security, privacy and comfort, while space connected them to different parts of the world, family and friends through social media.

Today, many young people define their identity from a global perspective. According to Avtar Brah (1996), 'identity is simultaneously subjective and social, and is constituted in and through culture, and culture and identity are inextricably linked concepts' (p.21). Culture played an important part in the writing group girls' lives; they identified with a more global teenage culture, connected with technology and social media, and they ascribed to being citizens of the world.

For many young people in contemporary Britain, place and space are global and not particularly fixed, as they move from place to place – from Yorkshire to Newcastle, from Jhelum in Pakistan to Spain, from their Rotherham streets to Burj Khalifa in Dubai. Young people move between virtual spaces and therefore develop fluid identities. The girls in the writing group had a more cosmopolitan identity, which linked further than just their parents' county of origin; this identity had been acquired through opportunities to travel and access to modern technology.

One participant writes about her annual visits to Dubai, where her cousin lives:

> My cousin is my tour guide,
> roaming around Dubai,
> Travelling to the Burj Kalifa,
> that is sky high

During 'Imagine' I was involved in another small-scale project called 'Threads of Time', funded by AHRC's Connected Communities Festival 2016. This project further explored identity and citizenship with the girls and allowed them to work with the local, Sheffield poet Helen Mort. The project examined British identity and the national narrative, cultural heritage, and how young people identify themselves. It explored the girls' links to the past, visualising a better future, and explored the effect of place on identity. This gave the young women the opportunity to reposition themselves, by defining their own citizenship, captured through a creative method. During the poetry workshops, Helen Mort read a poem, 'I come from' by Robert Seatter (2006). The girls took inspiration from Seatter's poem and wrote their own versions:

I come from
I come from a small a small island,
West Europe,
from the mountains of Scotland,
to the beeches in Butlins
I come from my saltiness of my chips,
made by good old Yorkshire

My mum is from Derby and my dad is from Newcastle.
I come from the blusher off my cheeks.
I come from My cherry lip balm.
I come from delicious chicken madras and from yummy fish
and chips.
I come from My nan's spicy mango chutney
I come from My neighbour's aromatic Spring rolls
and from My friends mouth-watering hummus

Many of the girls expressed how part of their global identity was linked to food. Food still plays an important part in British South Asian culture. It reinforces the importance of custom and traditions determined by rituals and religious beliefs that are connected to family life and community, such as Ramadan and fasting or weddings – even deaths. To the girls, their Pakistani cultural identity appeared to be important, as it tied them to their heritage and the past. Having roots, and valuing their personal histories, gave them stronger foundations to develop a more hybrid identity.

Singh-Ghuman (2010), in his study of 50 Asian youngsters in a multicultural school, found that young people were 'developing bi-cultural identities', adopting some societal norms but maintaining their own cultural and religious identities (p.327). Many Muslims feel unsure of where they belong. The need to belong and to be part of British society is important to them and often they felt like a jigsaw piece that never quite fits to make a complete picture. As Bourn argues, 'young people are in one sense citizens of a global culture but at the same time struggle for a sense of acceptance in the local societies in which they live' (2008, p.51).

We all want to feel a sense of belonging, but how far do we go to achieve it? I'm a British Pakistani; my grandparents settled in Britain. I value my Pakistani traditions but sometimes struggle to adapt to the British culture. I am culturally divided. I feel a sense of belonging because I was born here and see myself as no different to any other British young person of my age.

The downside to me having a mixed culture is that my parents sometimes clash religion and culture, which is really annoying as it limits me from enjoying a typical life of a British person. I'm not saying I want to forget about my Pakistani culture because I do find it cool in a way, like I'm different to all my mates but I feel like I deserve a little freedom.

The current generation's identity is negotiated between the local and global. As the girls contemplated a more global identity in their future, they wrote about their perfect global place. For example:

Welcome to our dream city, let us show you around.
Sky scrapers, taller than a giraffe;
towering above the ground.
It smells fresh like a forest after the rain.
You can travel by Unicorn, instead of a train.
Along the border beaches run for miles.
There is a look of acceptance in everyone's smile.
These softly lit streets do not discriminate,
you walk around them without fear of hate.
Every turn there is a maze of amazing food;
Mexican, Italian, Asian and more to suit your mood.
Shopping and reading on a perfect day,
watching a vivid sunset, shining gold on the bay.
It's a place everyone, has their say,
and that is why, we've decided to stay

Identity and religion

The young women I worked with were from Muslim families, and most had strong faith. Jacobson (1997) distinguishes between the ethnic and religious identity of the Pakistani Muslim community:

> Ethnicity is perceived as a matter of attachment to a set of traditions or customs from a place of origin, whilst religious identity, being a Muslim signifies belonging to a global community and commitment to a set of doctrines from the Quran and the Hadith.[3] (Jacobson, 1997, p.240)

Archer (2001) found that Muslim young men in British secondary schools were defining themselves in terms of their religious identity as opposed to their parents' country of birth, and that being 'Muslim supersedes nationality' (p.87). Muslim identity was also important to the girls in my study, heightened by the rise in Islamophobia in the West.

One of the participants wrote about her strong allegiance to Islam, but also acknowledged the difficulty of negotiating between two different cultures and different values, which are sometimes compatible but at other times clash. This can cause confusion and loss of place and sense of belonging.

I am a very strong-minded person because of my beliefs. I am a follower of Islam. That is the religion I was born into. I do have a passion for my grandparents' traditions from Pakistan. I also love following my ancestors' heritage culture as it has made me who I am now. However I was born in England so I have a right to also adapt to the British culture such as going to football matches and the seaside for fish and chips.

As Muslims, the girls advocated that Islam was a peaceful religion, and they condemned the violence and the terrorist acts they saw on television, which shocked and appalled them.

Islam is a religion of peace that is why it is the fastest growing religion. Indeed, one out of every five persons on this earth is a Muslim. There are nearly 3 million Muslims living in United Kingdom and the number is growing. Yet, unfortunately, Islam is also the most misunderstood of religions.

While working with these young women, I became more aware of the importance of self-identity to young people. Assimilation is leading to what Alba and Nee describe as the 'disappearance of an ethnic/ racial distinction and the cultural and social differences that expresses it' (Alba and Nee, 1997, p.863). One of the ways in which the Muslim girls in the writing group expressed their faith and identity was through wearing the hijab. They saw this as a strong part of their identity, which they wrote about. In the public arena, the hijab is heatedly debated, with some saying that it is anti-Western, unsociable, a sign of subservience and should be banned. The girls did not see wearing the hijab as being oppressive, but rather saw it as an act of defining themselves.

My hijab. My choice

As a British Muslim I wear the head scarf as it part of my faith (Islam) to cover my hair. I do not find it that hard as many girls wear the head scarf. I don't care what people think as everyone is different. Imagine if everyone was the same the world would be a boring place. When I started year 7, I was the only person who wore the hijab. I wasn't really comfortable but now I have got used to it. Nobody really says anything to me so I feel comfortable in it. Wearing it for 1 year and a couple of months I feel that it is a part of me. If I went out without my scarf I'd feel like there is something missing. I'm happy to wear the head scarf so if other people have an issue, it's their problem.

I am a practising Muslim; I go to the Mosque and learn how to read the Quran. My religion is not all about wearing the headscarf, praying and reading the Quran there is much more; it's also about respecting one another, forgiving people.

The reality for many Muslim young people today is that they suffer from intense hostility and suspicion. Yet despite this, the girls in my study found that Islam gave them comfort and a sense of purpose to their lives, and a way of coping with the racism and the rise in Islamophobia.

Identity and language

Some poets and writers have argued for the need to retain heritage, language, identity and the importance of these to minority ethnic communities. One such person is the dual-heritage Scottish writer and poet Jackie Kay. Jackie Kay was born to a Scottish mother and a Nigerian father. She was adopted as a baby by a white Scottish couple. In her writing, she explores the themes of identity, cultural differences and racism. Her books, *Adoption Papers* (1991), *Off Colour* (1997) and *Red Dust Road* (2011), are very powerful and capture the experiences of a dual-heritage woman.

Kay is proud of her Scottish roots, and promotes the retention of the Scottish language. She uses Scottish and Gaelic words and dialect, with rich rhythmic sounds and strong vowels. In her poem 'Fiere' (2011), meaning 'companion' or 'friend', she writes in her own dialect, which is so rich and pure that reading it makes one think: why should everything be in English? Translating something as beautiful as Kay's poems into English would dilute the passion of the poem, and the meanings of words would be lost in translation. Craith (2006) argues that 'we all identify with the mother tongue' (p.20) and that 'many nations have sought to cultivate a sense of belonging precisely through the promotion of a common language' (p.21).

In her poem 'Old Tongue' (2005), Kay grieves for the loss of her strong Scottish accent, lamenting that before we know it we lose important parts of ourselves and a sense of who we really are. When Kay was eight, she moved to the south of England. She mentions that she soon lost her Scottish accent and that it felt as if she had turned her back on Scotland on English soil, as her old words buried themselves.

The girls' writing group studied the work of Jackie Kay, and one participant wrote the following piece.

After reading Jackie Kay's poem 'In my country' I was very touched by it – identity is such a wide topic rarely discussed. We all want to feel a sense of belonging, but how far do we go to achieve it?

I'm a British Pakistani; I was born in England after my grandparents settled in Britain. I value my Pakistani traditions but sometimes struggle to adapt to the British culture. I wear the salwar kameez at home when surrounded by family but wear English modest dresses whilst out. I am culturally divided but still manage to feel a sense of belonging because I was born here and see myself as no different to any other British young person of my age.

One young woman also accepted that she could not master her mother tongue with ease, as she did other European languages. She acknowledges in her writing that this was a contentious issue with parents and grandparents:

> La calle de mi padre se llama 'Playa' significado 'beach' en Ingles.
> Ahora, estoy estudiando español.
> I learn European languages with ease, but I can't speak my mother tongue – Punjabi.
> What a disgrace I must be within the community
> But it's okay to embrace both my cultures, it's an honour to be British-Pakistani
> Now I've finally realised this, I am no longer confused.

The older generation in my community do feel a great sadness that many of their young people can no longer speak their mother language. Language is more than a tool for communication, 'it is a fundamental attribute to cultural identity and empowerment both for the individual and the group' (UNESCO, 2003, p.16).

Conclusion

Minority ethnic young people often successfully blend different cultural identities, and take the best from all culture. I believe that individuals who find a happy medium can contribute to society and to British life.

Parekh (2000) argues that the 'dominant definition of national identity can become a vehicle to mould the entire society in its image' (p.7). Appiah (2006) that 'people are different, the cosmopolitan knows, and there is much to learn from our differences. Because there are so many human possibilities worth exploring, we neither expect nor desire that every person or every society should converge on a single mode of life' (p.xv). Appiah was born to an English mother and a Ghanaian father, and he recollects his father saying to him and his sister to remember they were citizens of the world, which is how many young people view themselves.

Ward (2004) argues that: 'Britishness has always been unstable, it is always in the process of unravelling, rather than of forming a collective identity' (p.3). The girls in the writing group did not want to have the exact same identity as their parents, nor the same as their White peers; they are still very young and have time to construct their own ideal identity of Britishness, rather than being forced into it by policy makers' tick boxes. The young women saw a multicultural Britain – one that should recognise and accept their faith and culture.

Young people should be able to 'negotiate, manage, disagree and contest' their British identity' (Hopkins, 2010, p.6). Moulding the whole of society into one definition of national identity would be very hard to achieve, as it is not possible to force a particular identity on people and to take away their freedom to define themselves. Do young people from minority ethnic communities have to give up their culture, heritage and traditions, which link them to their parents' or grandparents' homeland, and become completely submerged in British culture in order to be accepted? It seems that would only weaken their identity. Ward (2004) argues: 'there is tension in all multiple identities but that does not make multiple identities fundamentally incompatible' (p.170).

Sir Keith Ajegbo, reviewing teaching of the diversity curriculum, commented 'that we all have a multiplicity of identities which may jostle with each other but which ultimately unite to make us individuals' (Ajegbo, 2007, p.29). This multiplicity of identities – and the way they intersect — was exemplified in the girls' writings and shows the girls exploring their identities as adult citizens of tomorrow.

Notes

[1]   I refer to the citizenship curriculum, driven by the UK government to create a unified citizenship, disregarding minority ethnic students' heritage and histories in favour of national identity, and slowly erasing other identities that might be important to young people, linked to their culture, language or religion.

[2]   The Osmonds are an American family music group with a number of hits in the 1970s. The Bay City Rollers are a Scottish pop band, whose popularity was at its height in the mid-1970s. *Jackie* was a British teenage magazine, which was highly popular in the 1970s.

[3]   Hadith is the book of narratives of the daily practices of the Prophet Mohammed, (PBUH) Peace Be Upon Him.

Part Three
Community ways of knowing

ELEVEN

Methodology: an introduction

Elizabeth Campbell

What counts for knowledge?

Part Three of this book explores the 'research methodology' that has shaped both the research and the writing of this book. Before we dive into that, though, we'll take a moment to define our terms. Lest the idea of research should sound intimidating, remember that we all do research every day. Shoppers compare prices, for example, students investigate courses, new parents watch others care for babies, teens try new games, and jobseekers weigh professional options.

At its most basic, *research* is a purposeful and systematic investigation that seeks to build new knowledge. The term *methodology* is a little trickier, but it can be thought of as the philosophies that researchers bring to their *research methods*, the tools that researchers use to do their work. These can include interviews, experiments, observations, surveys and much more.

In addition to these commonplace definitions, there are also a number of implicit – and often unspoken – ideas about what research is and how it should operate. Academically situated researchers undergo long training and socialisation processes that involve learning the forms, practices, traditions, theories and languages of their disciplines. As they move through those processes, they gain an expertise presumed to uniquely qualify them as researchers in that discipline. When these experts then produce knowledge, that knowledge is often endowed with a special authority; indeed, it is usually regarded as wholly different from the knowledge that those without academic credentials produce. Other researchers are more likely to draw, repeat or expand upon academically produced knowledge, and policy makers are more likely to put it to work. Moreover, because much academic knowledge is highly specialised, with its own technical terms or jargon, those who are not trained in academic language can have difficulty in reading and understanding that knowledge.

How do we make historical knowledge?

Before the mid- to late 20th century, it was not common for the people and communities being researched to have a say in how that research was conceptualised and carried out (Hymes, 1972; Asad, 1973), although many individual professional, academic or community-based researchers sought to work on more egalitarian terms with research participants (see, for example, Darnell, 2001; Lassiter, 2005; Oakley, 2017). In any case, until the 1970s and 1980s, it was more common for academic researchers to design and control research (Clifford, 1983). But as 'research subjects' – indigenous peoples, in particular – began to challenge academically produced representations of their cultures and traditions, some academic researchers responded by inviting those 'subjects' to participate throughout the research process, from developing research questions, to designing and implementing research studies, and interpreting, writing and presenting the research results (Lassiter, 2005).

As those developments progressed, the language of research began to change as well: terms such as 'consultant' or 'participant', which referenced expertise and collaboration, began to replace labels such as 'subject' or 'informant', which called up notions of passivity and one-way transfers of information (Oakley, 1981; Campbell and Lassiter, 2015). Questions about what kind of knowledge matters, and who should have a say in its production, arose and multiplied during the 1970s and 1980s, as did the range of innovative methodologies that sought to address them (see, for example, Brettell, 1993). Although these innovations remained largely at the margins of scholarly disciplines throughout the 1990s and into the 21st century, concepts of research as dialogic, reciprocal and collaborative became more widely understood and accepted (Lawless, 1992; Tedlock and Mannheim, 1995; Field, 2008). Those terms also named some of the ideas that lay at the heart of these innovative methodologies, which called for stronger attention to research equity, accuracy, ethics, purposes and audiences. Among the most important of these ideas were: the centrality of dialogue to knowledge production; the fundamental roles of reciprocity, ethics and relationships in social research; and the ideal of collaboration in research design and knowledge production (Lawless, 2000).

These ideas did not just emerge out of the ether. The impulse for more equitable and democratic forms of research grew out of, among other things, the gathering momentum of the 20th century's critique of colonialism (see, for example, Fanon, 1961; Said, 1979). During that time, more and more scholars began to name and describe the colonial ideals at the heart of so much knowledge production, and the colonial practices at the centre of so many research methodologies (Fabian, 1983; Spivak, 1988). In 1999, Linda Tuhiwai Smith offered a powerful critique of academic research, arguing that much of it – scientific and social scientific, especially – served not just to disempower local communities, but actually to harm them. Too many researchers and research projects, she charged, treated the experiences, traditions and even the bodies of indigenous people in the same way that colonialists had treated their lands: as resources to be mined and exploited.

Indigenous people, local communities and some researchers themselves began calling for different ways of thinking about and doing social science research. Over the last several decades, calls have increased for collaborative research that attends to, incorporates and even privileges the knowledge produced in and by non-academically situated people and communities (Lassiter, 2008). Across disciplines, researchers are exploring the legitimacy of knowledge produced by local experts, whether or not they are academically legitimised (Lassiter et al, 2004; Crow and Hart, 2012). These kinds of research proceed from different assumptions about how knowledge is produced: rather than framing knowledge as something out there that can be discovered or explained by external experts, these different notions of collaborative research instead see knowledge as something produced between different kinds of experts, engaged in intentional and meaningful interaction.

As more and more academically and community-situated researchers engage in collaborative research, ideas about what it is, how it works and why it matters are changing. Many of the early collaborative efforts emphasised consensus or accord, and were often framed in terms of agreement. But in the last couple of decades, notions of collaboration have begun to engage its complexity (Rappaport, 2008; Haviland, 2017). Rather than seeking and celebrating agreement, contemporary collaborations try to place differently produced knowledges alongside each other, acknowledging difference and the difficulties of working across it (Lassiter, forthcoming, a). In cases that range from indigenous councils in the Americas and Australia to the United Kingdom's 'impact agenda', collaboration as both practice and approach has become a requirement of social research.

Why does it matter?

Today's different forms of collaborative research proceed from the assumption that both community and academic researchers bring to the table different experience, knowledge and expertise, and that working together across those different positions can lead to new, relevant and potentially transformative knowledge about contemporary issues and challenges. Contemporary collaborative approaches also recognise that all researchers come from particular backgrounds and specific experiences; thus, neither they nor their research are presumed to be neutral. This book brings together a host of different – and differently situated – people, who are committed to a particular goal: to present a more complex (albeit, still tentative and partial) understanding of Rotherham and its people, the very diverse community at the heart of this text.

Collaborative methodologies recognise that all participants – regardless of training, credentials or situations – possess valid forms of knowledge and expertise. Collaborative methodologies ask researchers to work alongside research participants to co-produce knowledge that is mutually accessible and relevant. Embracing the actual human relationships at the centre of collaborative research opens all who participate to the possibility of being changed by each other.

Taken together, the chapters in Part Three ask readers to recognise our differing expertise and shared humanity, and to mobilise both of these in ways that can lead to deeper understandings of our very complex communities. We all want our communities to be better places. We want them to be better constituted, better informed, better prepared, and more able to meet the challenges of these increasingly complex times. If we are to meet those goals, we will have to find better ways of working together to identify, investigate and solve our common problems.

TWELVE

Collaborative ethnography
in context

Elizabeth Campbell, Luke Eric Lassiter and Kate Pahl

In this chapter, we write collaboratively about doing collaborative ethnography. We primarily draw on Eric and Beth's work over many years in establishing and developing the field of collaborative ethnography through their published work (see Lassiter et al, 2004; Lassiter, 2005; Lassiter and Campbell, 2010; Campbell and Lassiter, 2010; Campbell and Lassiter, 2015).

Bringing Eric and Beth to Rotherham from the US, and to the Rotherham team's encounter with them, through the support of Professor Graham Crow, was vital for the writing of this book. Graham Crow[1] is a Professor of Sociology and Methodology at the University of Edinburgh and was the original principle Investigator of the 'Imagine' project. We introduce collaborative ethnography as a methodology, but also describe the encounter that led to writing this book. This is a multi-voiced piece of writing, which begins with a discussion about the nature of research itself, and then moves on to describe the research encounter.

What are we doing when we do research?

Research methods are often presented in a 'how to' way. In this section, we muse on the way in which they are often taught, but then move on to a more philosophical discussion about the nature of research as a learning process. We begin by asking the question: What are we doing when we do research?

When people start out in doing research, very often they are introduced to 'research methods' courses, especially if they are studying at universities. These often explain the 'best way' of extracting information from people: through interviews, focus groups, surveys or participant observation. Very often, these courses teach a certain rubric. You start off with how to conduct an interview and develop a few practice questions. You work on defining your research question, before you go into the field. These courses tend to assume that the university researcher knows what they are doing, and that they know what they will find out, and how they will find it out. In my work, I (Kate) had previously worked in communities where I often did not know best how things should be. Even as a fledgling researcher, I was never very sure what I was going to find out, so these courses always seemed a little hard and other people seemed a lot more sure than I did as to what they would be doing.

When I returned to university as a graduate student interested in everyday literacy practices, I didn't know how to get started. I was lucky enough to have an anthropologist, Brian Street, as my supervisor. He suggested that I just go and hang out in places, take local buses and spend time talking to people and being with them. This 'method' was familiar to me as an outreach worker, and seemed a good way to go about doing things. Brian taught me about learning from people, and suggested, gently, that rather than 'study' the people I was interested in, I learned from them, and hung out with them, and then tried to figure out, with them, 'what is going on here'. He taught me that anthropology as a mode of research was itself a form of learning. Ingold (2014) identifies anthropology as a form of 'learning with' and that the only way to inhabit this space is to walk with people and to do things with people – being, making, understanding.

Learning is something we do together. Pedagogical spaces are often collaborative, involving shared inquiry and learning. As a team on this collaboration, we all work in educational settings. When we thought about collaborative ethnography, we realised that the kind of research we were doing is a form of collaborative pedagogy, where we learn together about the world, but also acknowledge each other's learning along the way. This idea of research might be seen more as a two-way process that involves dialogue, discussion, shared inquiry and collaboration – processes more often associated with being a student. We think that doing research is a lot like this; that it is a form of learning.

Who are we?

Our work, then, is a form of learning, and this chapter introduces you to us and to the learning we have done to write this book. We answer the question: Who are we?

Kate Pahl

Kate Pahl has a background in English and social anthropology, but also worked as an adult literacy outreach worker for many years. She became interested in communities and literacy practices through her work on estates in London, but then was also interested in ways in which literacy practices in homes and communities could be valued and understood within educational settings. Her books (see Pahl and Rowsell, 2010; Pahl and Rowsell, 2012; Pahl, 2014) focus on this central issue. Her work has valued everyday forms of knowledge production, and tries to make sense, through participatory methods, of what people recognise to be literate and what they do with literacy.

This work was often participatory and collaborative. Some of this book's authors helped Kate to understand how literacy could be seen differently through different eyes. These ways of knowing were constructed collaboratively, in libraries, with people, in the contexts in which they lived and worked. They led to the construction of new ontologies of literacy practices, which lay within the spaces of the home and the community and which did not derive from the disciplinary edifices in universities (see Finnegan, 2015).

The process of collaboration was created through people and with people. A number of projects – 'Writing in the home and in the street'; 'Language as talisman'; 'Communicating wisdom'[2] – were dreamed up through sitting in community centres with youth workers and young people. In more traditional research, these would possibly be seen as being the 'research subjects'. However, in the projects we were constructing, young people sat with us and helped to write the bids. They suggested ideas, they led us on our journey, and the process of making the research come alive was itself collaborative. This shaped how things evolved and how the 'Imagine' project was constructed. The projects drew on co-production as a methodology, with a particular focus on arts-based methods (see also Beebeejaun et al, 2014).

Beth Campbell and Eric Lassiter

Beth Campbell and Eric Lassiter have been thinking, practising and writing about collaborative ethnography since they first met, as graduate students, in a combined anthropology and folklore seminar entitled 'The art of ethnography'. Our (Beth and Eric's) Professor, Glenn Hinson – who served as chair for both Eric's Anthropology PhD dissertation and Beth's Folklore MA thesis – introduced us to collaborative ethnography as both an ideal and a practice. At the time, we thought of collaboration in the terms that Glenn used in *Fire in my bones*:

> True collaboration entails a sharing of authority and a sharing of visions. … Sharing authority and visions means inviting consultants to shape form, text, and intended audience. It also means directing the collaborative work toward multiple ends, ends that speak to different needs and different constituencies, ends that might be so differently defined as to have never even been considered by one or more of the collaborating parties. (Hinson, 2000, p.2)

We embraced collaboration in graduate school and practised it in our early careers for two primary reasons: first, because we believed collaborative work to be more morally and ethically sound; and second, because we believed that collaboration produced more accurate and equitable representations.

Much of Eric's early work centred on the expressive traditions of southwestern Oklahoma's Kiowa people. He worked with several Kiowa families to explore the experience and meaning of Kiowa songs and singing. In keeping with the notions of collaboration we held then, Eric and his collaborators worked together to select, define, carry out and disseminate their encounters with Kiowa song, from southern plains powwow singing, to peyote songs, to Kiowa Christian hymns (Lassiter, 1998; Lassiter et al, 2002). That work took a range of forms; although Eric and his collaborators did produce several books and other manuscripts, they also produced recordings, exhibitions and public events.

In 1996, Eric took a job with Ball State University, and he and Beth moved to Muncie, Indiana, home of the famous 'Middletown' studies.[3] While an assistant professor of anthropology, Eric honed his ideas about collaborative ethnography.

Beth took up community-based collaborative oral history, folklore and museum projects, and eventually took a job at a local museum, The Minnetrista Center. As part of an archaeology grant researching East Central Indiana's African American Pioneers, Beth interviewed pioneer descendants for an oral history project; those same descendants later became deeply involved in the conceptualisation and design of a museum exhibit that explored the stories of their ancestors. The first 'Other side of Middletown' project brought some of those people together with a team of museum staff and others from the community, to solicit early photographs of the city's African Americans. The relationships built in these early projects continued to grow. Many of those who were involved in that first 'Other side' project then became collaborators on *The other side of Middletown* (Lassiter et al, 2004), a collaborative ethnography involving well over 75 people, including local community members, students and faculty.

We learned a couple of key lessons in those early days. First, that deepening relationships[4] were emerging out of these multiple collaborations; and second, that these relationships, like all relationships, were both gratifying and complex. They could very well be defined by the affinity, rapport or agreement our initial ideals of collaboration hoped for; however, they could also be defined by discord, resistance or antagonism. To collaborate, we learned, is necessarily to engage difference. Engaging difference brings participants into complex relationships. Collaborations become sites for working across difference – *without eschewing it*. That's something we've been thinking about for quite some time.

What is collaborative ethnography?

During and after working on and writing *The other side of Middletown* (Lassiter et al, 2004), Eric began working on a new manuscript to outline the principles of collaborative ethnography. That manuscript eventually turned into *The Chicago guide to collaborative ethnography*, in which he defines collaborative ethnography as:

> an approach to ethnography that deliberately and explicitly emphasizes collaboration at every point in the ethnographic process, without veiling it—from project conceptualization, to fieldwork, and, especially, through the writing process. Collaborative ethnography invites commentary from our consultants and seeks to make that commentary overtly part of the ethnographic text as it develops. In turn, this negotiation is reintegrated back into the fieldwork process itself. Importantly, the process yields texts that are co-conceived or cowritten with local communities of collaborators and consider multiple audiences outside the confines of academic discourse, including local constituencies. (Lassiter, 2005, p.16)

This understanding of collaborative ethnography very much reflected how we (Beth and Eric) were thinking about collaborative ethnography at the time. It represents an evolution from where we started, and our thinking has continued to evolve. In the last decade or so, our ideas about collaborative ethnography – collaborative research of any stripe, really – have moved past tropes of agreement or consensus and towards developing more nuanced collaborations around articulations of difference. We'll come back to that.

Next, in an effort to offer a more nuanced take on collaborative ethnography that builds on the previous discussion, we:

- put forward what we see as the key principles of collaborative ethnography;
- very briefly review changes in collaborative ethnography over the past couple of decades;
- point to some of the potentials that we see for future work in collaborative ethnography.

The key principles

Most forms of collaborative ethnography mobilise the collaborative processes inherent in doing ethnography. Ethnographic activities like participant-observation or interviews necessarily rely on a kind of collaboration, of course. But collaborative ethnography places collaboration – deliberately and intentionally – at the centre of the ethnographic enterprise, making it a primary and explicit part of ethnographic practice from beginning to end. In collaborative ethnography, researchers – and here we refer to researchers across positions, from academics and artists to community development workers and interested citizens – work together to co-create research designs, collectively carry out the research, and, especially, co-produce the final ethnographic texts.[5]

This point is especially important to how collaborative ethnography is often understood and practised today: in traditional ethnography, a clear separation is often made between, on the one hand, the research carried out in the field (whatever and wherever that might be) and, on the other hand, the production of final texts. As we pointed out earlier, ethnographic fieldwork, by its very nature, often creates and/or draws upon intense and collaborative relationships. The texts that rise out of those relationships, however, are traditionally composed after the ethnographer has stepped out of the field. The lone ethnographer (or ethnographers, as in team ethnography) usually produces the ethnographic text in isolation, divorced from the collaborative relationships upon which the fieldwork depended. Collaborative ethnography actively seeks to collapse this separation, insisting that collaboration extend from the project inception and initial planning through the research and fieldwork and into the writing or production processes themselves (see Lassiter, 2005; Lassiter and Campbell, 2014).

One consequence of explicitly foregrounding collaboration is that the lines in traditional ethnography separating 'ethnographers' and 'subjects' (or 'informants', 'consultants' or 'participants') become less clear. Sometimes, they dissolve entirely. In collaborative work, each participant contributes different kinds of knowledge, expertise and authority, all of which become integral to the larger project. Concepts like 'the field' and 'valuable outcomes' become fuzzy, as do arguments over what might be considered 'research' (see, for example, Faubion and Marcus, 2009) and, perhaps most importantly, arguments over what counts for knowledge.

For researchers situated outside the academy, collaborative ethnography may present opportunities that range from filling in historical and representational gaps, to redressing past wrongs, to developing new collaboratively based activisms. For researchers situated within the academy, those opportunities are also present, although they are not without peril. Collaborative ethnography tends to challenge traditional scholarly authority; at the very least, it does not adhere to scholarly norms. These qualities are not always well received in academic circles.

Collaborative ethnographers embrace a number of different approaches, but in general, collaborative ethnography hinges on four key principles:

- First and foremost, collaborative ethnography emphasises and highlights the ethical and moral commitments between ethnographers and participants that frame the contours of a project. Our initial sense that collaborative ethnography was 'the right thing to do' is reflected in this first principle.
- Second, because negotiating common commitments (to research questions or outcomes, for example) are critical to the success of such projects, collaborative ethnographers must practise honesty and transparency with regard to research agendas, objectives and outcomes as they work through these processes.
- The third key principle builds on this: because collaborative ethnography works across multiple and diverse sites and audiences, accessible and dialogic writing (writing that seeks a middle ground between, for example, academic and community discourse) is engaged as a method for fostering discussion across diverse speech communities.

- Fourth and finally, collaborative writing and co-interpretation of developing ethnographic texts becomes central to developing final products from beginning to end. (see Lassiter, 2005, pp. 77-154)

These key principles represent, of course, an ideal that is not always easily attained. Although the impulses for valuing and doing collaborative ethnography run deep (see Lassiter, 2005, Part I), collaborative ethnography continues to develop and evolve.

Changes in collaborative ethnography

Over the past two decades, a critical literature about collaboration in general, and collaborative ethnography in particular, has emerged, and a host of ethnographers and research participants have explored new and exciting contexts for doing collaborative ethnography, from video to art to teaching. (Many such examples can be found in the journal *Collaborative Anthropologies*.)

One of the most important developments in collaborative ethnography to have emerged in the last two decades is a focus on difference and negotiation. Again, when we first started doing collaborative ethnography, our focus tended to be on finding grounds for agreement and similarity, on those values or happenings that bring projects together and about which participants agree, or (at the very least) are willing to engage. But, as we observe in *Doing ethnography today* (Lassiter and Campbell, 2015, pp.21-3), when people work together towards a cooperatively imagined outcome, relationships, histories, ethical and moral choices and commitments, personal sensibilities and aspirations, ideas and assumptions inevitably collide. The more deeply researchers – again, across identities and positions – engage in collaborative work, the more likely they are to recognise its multiple possibilities and tensions and to understand its very complex nature.

More and more, ethnographers are investigating how participants work with and across difference in collaborative projects. This makes sense, of course; attending to the human relationships upon which collaborative ethnography depends inevitably exposes both similarity and difference, and reveals both shared and conflicting aims. If being honest and transparent is critical to the success of collaborative projects, as we believe that it is, then being honest about how collaboration works is equally critical. This means that we must find ways to engage the actual differences we encounter when doing this work.

Collaborative ethnographers are thus increasingly interested in elaborating the actual mechanics of collaboration, the ebbs and flows of the process. Attention to collaboration's complexity and dynamism focuses our attention not on what we wish collaboration to be, but on the actual complications of doing collaborative ethnography in the present. Today's collaborative ethnographers are less interested in 'models' for doing collaborative ethnography and are more interested in elaborating the unique contexts in which collaborative projects unfold, which often means paying very close attention to how particular relationships engender very particular kinds of collaborative projects (Lassiter forthcoming, a; Lassiter forthcoming, b).

Potentials for future work in collaborative ethnography

Contemporary collaborative ethnographers have also begun asking important questions about the work itself, such as:

- Can there be a more critical collaborative ethnography (see, for example, Bhattacharya, 2008; Breunlin and Regis, 2009)?
- How might we mobilise newer forms of collaborative ethnography (texts or action, for example) more effectively?
- What might we do with these new forms of ethnography as they continue to unfold (see Lassiter and Campbell, 2010)?

A central development has included a focus on the pedagogy of ethnography as a site of knowledge reproduction: in the university at both graduate and undergraduate levels (see Holmes and Marcus, 2008; Campbell and Lassiter, 2010; Hyatt, 2013); and in the communities where collaborative ethnography and other forms of collaborative research surface (Crow and Hart, 2012).

Collaborative ethnography and Rotherham

In the Rotherham project, collaborative ethnography became a way of closing the distance between those who write about people and those who are written about. It made explicit the discussions and debates that happen when we learn together, but it also went further. For us, collaborative ethnography is about not only understanding things collaboratively, but also writing about them and producing them collaboratively – hence this book.

The process involves a commitment to relationships, to moral responsibility, to sharing and to time spent with people. In working on this book, Eric and Beth came over from the US to the UK, to meet with the people who co-authored this book. In the following vignettes, first Kate writes about that experience and the effect that it had on her as a researcher; then Beth and Eric follow with the same story from their perspective.

Kate's view: encountering the field

I am always nervous when doing a new thing. I was especially nervous on the morning of 3 September 2015. A long while ago, when I was planning the 'Imagine' project, I sat with Professor Graham Crow, who originally developed and led the 'Imagine' team. Graham asked me if I liked the work of Eric Lassiter. 'Oh I love that book!' I said, enthusiastically, and indeed Eric's book from 2005 was eagerly read and reread as I embarked on trying to do things in ways that were consultative, participatory and involved co-writing and co-authoring (see Pahl and Pool, 2011).

I had encountered his work with Beth in recent articles (Campbell and Lassiter, 2010), because it expressed so clearly the dilemmas I myself was encountering while doing work in Rotherham. It seemed another kind of work, engaged, continual and committed to changing things in communities. Graham Crow had actually managed to get Eric and Beth onto our project and they were coming over from the US to meet me in Rotherham, and the partners I worked with. I was convinced something would go wrong. The endless angst over writing a book about Rotherham seemed risky and uncertain.

So 3 September was not only about two American academics coming over to meet the team; there was also the team. As represented in this book, we were a group of people united in a common purpose, which was, in some ways, to represent in a positive light the cultures and histories of a place that had traditionally not been represented in the best light; but also we wanted to re-imagine collective futures – and better futures together. Our projects were focused on culture, on writing in the community, on portraits of British Muslims, on histories and hopes and fears and dreams. We wanted to make sure that our voices were heard, in an era when many communities were not being heard.

However, in the back of my mind, the most important thing was that there was to be a book. In the spirit of *The other side of Middletown* (Lassiter et al, 2004), we would write a book that 'set the record straight'. People from the town of Rotherham could have a chance to refute the accounts by Charlesworth (2000) and Baggini (2007) and to write their own book, about their own town – the town they lived in. In our book we would write a 'Middletown study' that could add to the literature, 'that gives a "face" to the people who live here;

that situates this place in real people's experience' (Lassiter et al, 2004, p.22). We had said we would write this book in our grant proposal, and I was determined that we should do this.

On 3 September, I picked up Eric and Beth from their hotel, feeling a bit scared. I was interested in what they thought they were doing here, and what they really were intending to do. In the car on the way to Rotherham, we talked about 'service learning' and the need we all seemed to have to contribute, to be part of, and to be active within communities. Eric talked about the museum trust he was part of; Beth talked of her students and of the value she placed on the processes of writing and making sense together. Slowly I realised that here were two people who genuinely knew that this stuff was messy and chaotic, but who liked doing it; they enjoyed not knowing what was going to happen next and they liked being in the car with me. I began to relax.

Our meeting went very well. People came and talked:

- Deborah came and told us about her literacy project, 'Grimm and Co', and about the community project she was creating in the town centre, a storyshop.
- Zahir came and told us about his portraits and his vision for a new vision, based on his portraits, for British Muslims, drawing on the everyday.
- Khalida and Cassie came and told us about art as a space of hope and inspiration.
- Zanib came and explained about her vision for a book that would acknowledge identities, histories, experiences.
- Mariam came and told us about her historical research into her father's history in the British navy.
- Paul Ward and Elizabeth Pente came and gave us support in relation to the history of the project and how we could buttress it with research on 'British-ness' and identity.

At one point, I wished I had an audio recorder and could record the discussions — they were so rich. We disagreed at times, but everyone acknowledged that it was a satisfying encounter. Two weeks later, I had the book proposal ready to send off to the publisher. I had achieved my aim.

In the car on the way back to Sheffield, I said that I was relieved that it had gone well. Beth said that Eric was always nervous about the research product. I said I was too. Beth said, but it's the process that matters; it's the listening to and learning from each other, the being and doing together, the struggling through it all that counts. This had never occurred to me. I had been focused on this book as a product, but in the meantime, things had happened, we had learned together – and that seemed to be a very important part of doing collaborative ethnography.

Beth and Eric's view: encountering Rotherham

We flew into Nottingham on 2 September 2015, and had a very friendly and easy dinner in Sheffield that evening with Kate Pahl, Steve Pool, and Kim Streets. The next day, we met the full team at MyPlace Rotherham, a YMCA building made of sharp angles, bright colours and clear glass. We were nervous too, quite frankly; we kept getting the sense that a lot was riding on our visit but we weren't quite sure what ... or why. Fortunately, at least in Beth's case, jet lag overrode nervousness.

One of the main points of the day's conversation was whether and how the group could co-produce a text that reflected their shared experiences and different perspectives. They seemed tentative and unsure to us, that when it came to this collaborative ethnography stuff, they did not quite know what they were doing. Beth was taken aback by that uncertainty; it seemed that the group was asking whether or not they could write a collaborative ethnography, when it was pretty clear that they were already in the middle of it.

The team knew our *The other side of Middletown* work (Lassiter et al, 2004), and were trying to find a way to transfer what we had done in Muncie, Indiana, to what they were doing in Rotherham. But one of the things we've learned since *Middletown* is that there isn't a way to do the same thing twice. There is no way to model collaboration. We did not know it at the time, but the collaborative ethnography we undertook in *Middletown* was the first and last time we'd ever be able to collaborate in that precise way. Every collaboration is situational and particular; each is grounded in distinct times and places; engages specific relationships and resources; and navigates specific issues and agendas. The Rotherham team shared a commitment to their project, but they were negotiating difference and building relationships in their own situated and particular ways. That's the key to any successful collaborative project.

Eric was struck by the very profound differences between team members – in terms of gender, ethnicity, religion, profession, position, training, mode of expression, reason for participating in the project and more – but also the very clear similarities and shared commitments that brought them together. Kate had told us about a recent crisis in the project, in which some of those differences had more or less blown up, which had led several members to leave the collaboration. It was a difficult time for the team, extraordinarily difficult for some. Kate had been left reeling; as the project lead, she'd felt as though she had failed. But crises and blow-ups are real possibilities in collaborative work. Relationships do break down; sometimes in pretty spectacular ways. What was interesting – and inspiring – about this project is that it broke down, and then was reconstituted. They were still working with and across real differences in very explicit and profound ways. What Eric was most curious about was whether they were going to try to gloss over those differences, or mobilise them as a critical part of how they talked about and did their collaborative work.

Although the differences that had been irreconcilable were no longer present, real differences remained, and the Rotherham team had an opportunity to place themselves and their project right at the edge of how collaboration works. Too often, the literature on collaborative work evades its difficulty. The frictions and ruptures that so often accompany collaboration are avoided, as if they were failures. Or set aside, as if they were not relevant. We did both in *The other side of Middletown*; at the time, we did not fully grasp how 'natural' difference, friction and rupture were to collaboration. Until very recently, the evasion we practised in *Middletown* has characterised the narrative framework for talking about collaborative work. It is different now. Today, people are talking about collaboration via rupture, via friction, via problems and differences; the Rotherham team has the opportunity to be in this new strand of literature. What we'd read and discussed in preparation for our visit to Rotherham, and what we'd heard described that day, was a very clear example of how collaboration actually works.

Late in the afternoon, Eric reflected on what a great opportunity this was to watch and be part of a project that was pushing in these familiar but novel directions. They are familiar in the sense that they are collaborative projects, and novel in that they are focusing on difference, and on places of not necessarily rupture, but perhaps dissonance. There are all of these persons and ideas and themes and agendas at work here. Although they do not always line up or match, it is clear that they are all still a part of the same thing.

Putting collaboration to work?

So here, we reflect together on what we have learned from each other, but also what we have learned by working collaboratively with communities. In our projects, we have also learned to let go. We have learned that other people generally know best, and they might have much more to contribute than we do on specific topics that they generally know more about than us. As Steve Pool says in his manifesto on artists and studio practice[6]:

> The studio is a conceptual space where groups form and grow things.
>
> - It emerges from something we recognise as working already.
> - It involves a group of people who operate beyond the structures of the university.
> - It transcends individual projects.
> - It recognises different types of expertise – all participants can emerge as 'experts'.
> - It does not assume that universities 'know best'.
> - It is acknowledged, however, that people in universities do know something. (with thanks to Steve Pool)

We write about our experience of collaborative ethnography in order to better understand what it is and to present the practice to other people who might want to do the same thing. We cannot pretend to know all the answers, but we have tried and, in trying, have come up with the kind of hard answers reflected in this quote:

> Once the inevitabilities are challenged, we begin gathering our resources for a journey of hope. If there are no easy answers there are still available and discoverable hard answers and it is these that we can now learn to make and share. This has been, from the beginning, the sense and the impulse of the Long Revolution. (Williams, 1985, pp.268-9)

We realised as we worked together that there are aspects of collaborative ethnographic practice that we think are important to highlight:

- We recognised that this work was multi-vocal and represents voices in different ways, often not producing one, clearly authored, narrative.
- We saw that it happened within meetings, and in shared discussions. It involves public pedagogy, and learning in informal and formal settings, and is always contested and contingent upon experience.

- We saw that it was located within ideologies of care and commitment. It has links with ideas such as service learning, and it is often about practice, about being there, witnessing, spending time with people, and not just sitting in the university.
- We also saw that it was process led. Most important, it is about the journey, the process, the learning – and less about the product.

Reflection

So what does this all mean? In a recent Skype call between the three of us, we discussed what we would write in this chapter. Kate talked about some work she had been doing on evaluating collaborative interdisciplinary projects. We realised that we needed to articulate what this stuff was, but in doing so, we also needed to describe it in ways that make sense. Beth talked about neo-expressivism – a radical openness to storied ways of knowing and to people's own experience, a genuinely situated form of knowledge creation. Eric talked about rhizome and the work of Deleuze.

At the beginning of this chapter, Kate talked about the learning together that lives at the heart of research, and pointed to the link between collaborative ethnography and collaborative pedagogy. Beth and Eric explored that link, too, in writing about 'the relationship of collaborative ethnography to modes of collaborative engagement and collaborative pedagogy – processes by which faculty, students, and members of local communities work as partners in an enlarged community of co-learners, co-researchers, and, especially, co-citizens' (Campbell and Lassiter, 2010, p. 370). That link emerged after the Middletown project, and has become clearer and clearer ever since.

In the same way that collaborative ethnography disrupts traditional divisions between community and university, and between researchers and the researched, collaborative pedagogy disrupts the traditional division between teacher and student. At the core of both collaborative ethnography and collaborative pedagogy are three things:

- a shared commitment between collaborators;
- the belief that all bring valuable knowledge to the table;
- a willingness to work across difference.

The longer we sit with and practise these ideas, the clearer the links between collaborative ethnography and collaborative pedagogy become. We have come to see that collaborative ethnography and collaborative pedagogy are intertwined, if not identical. At the very least, they are animated by the same spirit. In both, we learn together about the world and acknowledge each other's learning along the way. Collaborative research really is a form of collaborative teaching and learning.

Notes

[1] We would like to thank Professor Graham Crow for enabling this collaboration to happen.

[2] These were all funded through the Arts and Humanities Research Council 'Connected communities' programme.

[3] Muncie, Indiana was made famous by Robert S. Lynd and Helen Merrell Lynd's *Middletown: A Study in American Culture* (1929), which set off subsequent studies of 'Middletown' that last to this day.

[4] We are referring here to human relationships, but it is equally important to think about the other kinds of relationships that emerge out of collaboration – institutional, political, disciplinary, and so on.

[5] We use the term 'text' to refer to those products, but apply that term very broadly, from printed publications to digital presentations to public events.

[6] See 'The Manifesto' by The Polytechnic: www.poly-technic.co.uk.

THIRTEEN

Safe spaces and community activism

Zanib Rasool

I have long experience of community development and consider that it is still as important today as it was in the 1970s and 1980s for empowering women. Policy makers should refocus on the voice of women who are marginalised, and create safe spaces for women to develop their skills in a nurturing environment; we need to put gender back on the agenda. I see the community as an important knowledge base through its various assets and networks, which are being underused and undervalued. Everyone has something to offer.

The 1990s saw a decline in community development due to lack of funded posts and a lack of capacity building and training opportunities, as well as changed funding priorities, which lead to community disempowerment and professionals 'doing things to communities', creating a culture of dependency. In times of austerity the state now once again looks to communities for solutions to social, economic, and environment issues.

Checkoway argues that:

> Community development is a process in which people join together and develop programs at the community level. It can find its expression in geographical places where people reside, in groups whose members have similar characteristics, and in causes that people share in common. (2013, p.473)

In the UK, community development was inspired by three traditions dating back to the 19th century, as Gilchrist (2009, pp.24-25) explains:

- self-help groups offering neighbourly support during hardship;
- sharing resources through organisations such as trade unions;

- voluntary service to improve the lives of the disadvantaged, which by the 1970s was influenced by radical community and collective activism.

The 1990s saw a decline in community development due to a lack of funding for posts, a lack of training being offered, changing funding priorities and government policies. However, community development is now back on the agenda again through the work of the Department of Communities and Local Government (DCLG), who want to give more power back to local neighbourhoods and communities in order for them to have a bigger say on local issues, participate in decision making and design and deliver services themselves.

The history of community development in Rotherham

Britain's steel industry brought Pakistani/Kashmiri families like mine to Rotherham seeking work in the 1960s. More women joined their husbands here in the 1970s. In the early 1980s, there was a demand for new services and provision that could support the specific needs of the Pakistani community, especially the women. These required people from the same background, who could understand the language and cultural issues, to act as mediators between the individual and the existing generic services – someone to advocate for them.

This led to the setting up of dedicated Black and minority ethnic organisations. The Multi-Cultural Centre was set up in Rotherham in the early 1980s, to support Pakistani women's education and training, with a number of activities taking place in a small terraced house that became a thriving community hub:

> When I came to Rotherham there was not a single Asian woman seen on the street. I set up the Multi-Cultural Centre as women were isolated in the home, and there was nothing for women to do. The aim was to empower women and enable others to recognise the potential of women within the British Asian community. (Interview with founder member)

The centre provided a network for minority women, many of whom were new to this country and had left behind family and friends. In the 1980s, Black and Asian women leaders across the UK started establishing their own organisations, to tackle issues that women in their communities faced, such as low-level education, domestic violence and health issues. These organisations advocated for minority women and challenged inequalities. They became a collective voice for marginalised women.

My story

I started working at the Multi-Cultural Centre in the mid-1980s as a trainee community development worker. This early experience of community development work gave me a good grounding for my future work in the voluntary sector. I was undertaking face-to-face work with community members and groups, and I gained valuable insight into human interactions and everyday social relationships and practices. It was a safe space for me and other young women to develop our community knowledge and skills, and to learn community work.

According to Conteh and Brock (2010): 'Safe spaces are teaching and learning spaces where culture is co-constructed and mediated, where people create opportunities for themselves for meaning making and identity construction through language and social tools' (p.349). Jackson (2010) argues that social spaces can enhance a sense of belonging for migrant women and where they can 'develop a relational understanding of different ways of knowing as well as replacing knowledge lost through depletion of familial networks' (p.249).

As community development workers, we facilitated the participation of women in education and learning. That involved outreach and knocking on endless doors, to encourage women who lacked confidence to join an ESOL (English as second language) class we were running or to attend a women's health information event. Sadly, many community development workers of the 1980s have retired, leaving a large skills gap and taking with them a vast knowledge about their communities.

Reflecting on my experience of community development, I wrote this poem:

The old dinosaurs
It's so sad to see them go, the battle axes who tried to free women from the slavery of the kitchen sink, now almost extinct
Door knocking in the rain, walking for miles on the same street, and getting the same welcome as the rent collector but that did not deter them

> Forcing open the floodgates of learning, encouraging thirst for knowledge whilst you ironed and changed endless nappies

Women's activism tends to be around local issues of geographical or community interest, such as green spaces for children to play, traffic issues near a school, or the closure of community libraries or youth centres. As Susan Hyatt says, 'the most important and interesting activism occurred in women's homes as part of their everyday lives' (Hyatt, 2014).

Women often come into activism to protect their family and community interests. Brown and Ferguson (1995), commenting on women's activism on toxic water, argue that: 'Grassroots activists involved in toxic waste issues have most often been women' (p.145). They noticed that most of those women activists were housewives from working-class or lower-middle-class backgrounds, and most had never been political activists until they discovered the threat of toxic contamination in their communities (Brown and Ferguson (1995, p.146).

Community development and networks: a case study

An important aspect to community development is to look at all the resources in our community that go untapped – the buildings that are under-used, people with skills and knowledge to share. Mathie and Cunningham (2003) point to the valuable resources that already exist in our neighbourhoods:

> Communities are helped to build an inventory of their assets and are encouraged to see value in resources that would otherwise have been ignored, unrealised, or dismissed. Such unrealised resources include not only personal attributes and skills but also the relationships among people through social, kinship, or associational networks. (Mathie and Cunningham, 2003, p.476)

A local library and a school provide valuable access for women in Rotherham to take part in first step learning, including courses on sewing, information technology, English language, and exercise and fitness. There are passionate women in Rotherham, who want to make a difference to the lives of other women. They are charismatic leaders that inspire other women in their community to aim higher.

Empowering women: activism through writing and community learning

Women in the community need role models – individuals from either the local or global sphere from whom they can learn. Hoyt and Simon (2011) undertook a research project on the impact of role models on women's leadership and aspirations. They suggest that: 'female leaders who explicitly disconfirm the negative self-relevant stereotype and with whom people strongly identify have a more positive impact on women' (p.33). This was true for the girls' writing group I worked with. They looked for role models from minority ethnic backgrounds that they can aspire to be like, such as Rosa Parks or Malala Yousafzai.

The following writing is from Lucy, one of the young participants of the 'Threads of Time' project based in Rotherham. Writing has built her confidence, and her bedroom has now become her safe writing space. Lucy writes:

> My role models fought against poverty, sexism, inequality, racism, and male patriarchal structures. They had the courage and determination to reach their goal, they were strong, independent women; and girls like myself from minority backgrounds, need to discover our role models that fit with our ethnic and cultural identity.

Another group of women in Rotherham produced a herbal remedy book, sharing family herbal remedies passed from one generation of women to another for various ailments. The following is a selection of the remedies shared by the group:

Healing broken bones
Hot milk with Turmeric powder

Migraine
Cut thick slice of raw potatoes and wrap in muslin cloth, place on forehead where the pain is

Sore throat
Honey and lemon mixed with orange juice

The women volunteers who have gained skills at the local school now come back and teach the other women in their community craft and sewing skills, passing on creative knowledge.

Communities as funds of knowledge

The 'Imagine' project research team was able to feed in some of our findings to the UK government's funding policy via meetings with the DCLG. I shared my experience of community development and argued that the community library and school activities (mentioned earlier) can have a long-term impact on women in the community. These approaches build on communities' knowledge and capacity, by utilising skills that already exist in those communities. Not all knowledge can be found in books; ordinary women in communities hold a wealth of lived knowledge that needs to be shared. Women provide informal counselling, mentoring and financial advice to friends and community members, and have a wealth of experience.

Small scale neighbourhood projects can have much bigger impact due to an asset-based approach. For example, some of the participants in the community library writing group have gone on to set up a sewing group in the community library and to share their skills. Many people in the community who have limited household budgets now need to learn to make clothes due to welfare reform. Torri (2012) looked at community-based enterprise in rural India and mentions 'group approach and "networking" in enhancing the gender development through entrepreneurship activities' (p.58). The same entrepreneurial activities also exist in some of our poorer neighbourhoods, but often such enterprise goes unrecognised by policy makers.

Communities are 'funds of knowledge', a term used by Gonzalez et al (1999), referring to 'historically developed and accumulated strategies (that is, skills, abilities, ideas and practices) or bodies of knowledge that are essential in a household's functioning and wellbeing' (p.3). Women have a number of skills that need to be nurtured and utilised for the betterment of those communities. Gonzalez et al (1999) explore how families develop social networks that interconnect them with their environment and other households, and how those social relationships facilitate the development and exchange of resources, including funds of knowledge (p.3).

Women need strong networks to support each other, to learn from one another and to be a collective voice. Gilchrist (2009) states that: 'Community Development supports networks that foster mutual learning and shared commitment so that people can work and live together in relatively coherent and equitable communities' (p.21).

Ways forward: implications for policy and practice

We need to open up underused community buildings, such as community centres, and utilise existing knowledge and skills in communities to meet local needs, such as the isolation of elders, youth nuisance, and health issues, to name but a few. Community libraries, church halls, mosques, schools and community centres need to be made accessible, so that women's activism can be nurtured. A good example is the community library writing group, which was attended by women of all abilities and those with little or no English. They could still write poetry that was translated into English – and some were really good poets.

John Cavaye argues that, 'Community development means that a community itself engages in a process aimed at improving the social, economic and environmental situations of the community' (n.d, p.1). A good example of this comes from the organisation that I work for, Rotherham United Community Sports Trust, who have been supporting isolated 55-plus older male fans to set themselves up as a small community network that is volunteer led. They run weekly football reminiscence and walking football sessions; they organise their own away days and walking football competitions across the region. It is a low cost community initiative that benefits more than 60 men each week.

Community development work should be about giving local people the tools to become change makers, by unlocking community potential at neighbourhood level. Benenson and Stagg (2015) argue that: 'asset based approaches build on the capabilities, strength, and skills of lower income individuals and their neighbourhood institutions' (p.135). We tend to stigmatise deprived neighbourhoods, by overlooking the capabilities of individuals who live there. By doing this, we lose out on the wealth of knowledge and skills, as we tend to work with communities from a 'deficit model', by undermining the assets that already exist in those communities – people, the knowledge and skills, as well as other assets.

I see safe spaces as being enshrined in the everyday, where new knowledge is being created and shared. We need to change how we think about communities and how we work with communities – and we need to reposition communities as agents of for change.

FOURTEEN

Emotions in
community research

Zanib Rasool

My work involves using visual arts and narrative to explore women's lives; I also use creative writing and oral history in order to engage communities in arts practice, community histories and co-production. I was involved in the writing element of the 'Imagine' project, working with three writing groups in Rotherham. I never imagined that emotions would play such a pivotal role in this research project. Sara Ahmed (2004) describes emotions as 'involving bodily processes of affecting and being affected by objects and things' (p.208) and thinking about those objects can bring up certain feelings of pain, anger or happiness.

In academic social science, emotions have 'historically been associated with the irrational and quite opposed to the objective scientific search for knowledge' (Holland, 2007, p.196). However, in the last decade or so, sociologists have recognised that ethnographic research cannot be clinical and detached from human emotions. As Stodulka (2014) argues: 'Ethnographers' emotions are valuable data when conducting research with marginalised communities. Ethnographers' emotions contribute to, rather than compromise his or her understanding and theorising of our interlocutors' local worlds' (p.84).

My role in the writing group was participatory. I took part in the reading and writing of poetry and sharing my own experiences with the group. As someone who has worked in the Rotherham community for a long time, I know that when you interact with people, there will be a reciprocal relationship of human feelings. Godwin et al (2001) argue that 'emotions are part of the "stuff" connecting human beings to each other and the world around them' (Petray, 2012, p.556). Sara Ahmed (2004) states: 'Emotions are associated with women, who are represented as "closer" to nature'; she argues that 'some emotions are elevated as signs of cultivation, whilst others remain "lower" as signs of weakness' (p.3).

Writing connects ordinary women and gives them the opportunity to articulate feelings not expressed or shared before. We can say 'emotions do things' – they move us but also connect us with others. I argue that emotions help people with 'meaning making', and offer different experiences of the world through a different lens.

Writing through a woman's lens

Under the 'Imagine' project, we set up three writing groups: one in a community library; one in a women's group at a school; and a poetry group for young women aged 11 to 17 delivered in community venues. Setting up these groups was the best methodology for engaging women and young girls from minority communities, who felt more comfortable articulating their experiences through written words.

At our weekly community library sessions, the women's group shared and wrote about emotive subjects. McLoughlin (2003) argues that 'the processes of perception are deeply rooted in emotions about the self, about the external world and in cultural ways of seeing the world' (p.67). Emotions help you with 'meaning making' of your world and offer you another lens through which to view the social world you inhabit. Women from different backgrounds joined, which added to the diversity and dynamics of the group. The group was inclusive; those women who could not write in English could write and read in their own mother language and we interpreted for each other. As women, we have so much in common and share certain experiences. Our conversation led to certain themes that came out of the writing groups and included:

- gender inequality (education, employment, domestic role);
- education (barriers to learning, stereotyping of roles);
- identity (being British, racism);
- making sacrifices (caring responsibilities, giving up careers);
- mental and physical health (wellbeing of women);
- faith and spiritualism (different beliefs);
- nature and human life (living, old age and dying).

In my field notes, I wrote:

> Writing is a channel for migrant women and British-born women of ethnic minority background to express their voice of discontent in a culture where women are not expected to voice their opinions too loudly. Through writing, they can

challenge gender inequality, discrimination and patriotism; writing empowers women and gives a voice to the voiceless. We shared our very personal life journeys through stories, writing and poetry and celebrated our inner strength as women and the instinct for survival, for we are survivors. Poverty, violence, oppression, discrimination, broken marriage whatever life throw at us, we get up again.

Godwin and Jasper (2001) wrote that: 'Women's emotions (and those of other powerless groups like racial and ethnic minorities, the disabled) are often characterised in ways that blunt their challenges to authorities or cultural norms' (p.618).

During the 'Imagine' project research, the research team also discussed some of their personal experiences – whether it was barriers they faced in education or inequality in the workplace. I called the women's library writing group the 'sisterhood group'. As all three groups gelled, they became more open to revealing their feelings and emotions, as we established a relationship of trust, based on mutual respect. My field notes reflect this:

> At our sisterhood group, we encourage and praise each other in female solidarity and over time the women in the group have become bolder and more confident in their writing and sharing with each other their very personal piece of writing. We are all "sensitive souls" that have come together from different walks of life to the safe haven of the community library.

Many studies have shown writing to be therapeutic after a traumatic event. For example, Smyth (2001) writes:

> writing is the act of converting emotions and images into words which changes the way the person organises and thinks about the trauma. Once in narrative formation, the event can be summarised, stored and assimilated more efficiently, thereby reducing the distress associated with the traumatic experience. (Smyth, 2001, p.162)

The writing groups created a female network. Stean (2006) suggests that solidarity might be 'founded on the basis of shared principles and/ or generated by feelings of empathy towards other members of the group' (Gray, 2011, p.210). The library sessions were particularly close to my heart, as they nurtured my creative skills; before those Thursday morning sessions, I never wrote poetry. From a feminist stance, the writing sessions explored gender inequality and patriarchy, and that globally as women we are still struggling in all arenas of life – both public and private.

Refocusing research to incorporate new events

Things happen during research that you may have not planned for. When working with communities, you have to be flexible and to adapt the research to emerging themes and changes.

The Jay Report (Jay, 2014) (mentioned earlier in Chapter Three) was one such thing, and the focus of the research changed to take into account the impact on the everyday experiences of the people we were working with. This report led to a strong emotional tide and shock, which affected the participants of the writing group and everyone around them. They felt vulnerable and very tearful, which led to some of the group members writing and capturing the immediate emotions they were experiencing at that moment in time and place.

Field notes are essential for this kind of research. They enable you to record your own feelings at that time and in that space, which you can reflect on later. Campbell and Lassiter (2015) undertook an ethnographic study of Indiana's county fairs in the United States. Eric Lassiter stressed the importance of taking field notes during research and argued that, 'notes represent a snapshot, a fleeting intersection of time, place, persons, and events viewed through a very specific and particular lens of experience' (Campbell and Lassiter, 2015, p.54).

As a community researcher, you do feel emotional if you live through the same traumatic experiences as the participants of your research day in and day out; you cannot remain totally objective. Some of the girls' and women's lived experience during the period of the research was in the context of the sexual exploitation and abuse reported in the Jay Report, as well as the aftermath – and that was then reflected in their writing.

Women writers as role models

The women had a visit from our guest poet, Debjani Chatterjee MBE, an amazing and inspirational woman, whose poetry the group related to. We read some of her poems, which inspired the group to attempt writing themselves. Debjani read one of her poems, 'I was that woman', which describes the perils and pains of being a woman, expected to live a life of servitude and punishment.

For additional inspiration, we also explored the work of two South Asian poets at our sessions. The first was Parveen Shakir, who, through poetry, wrote about social taboos, domestic violence, gender inequality, patriotism and discrimination. The other was Sarojini Naidu, known as the 'Nightingale of India', who also challenged male domination and patriarchy. The emotional tide of their poetry stayed with us and inspired the women attending the library sessions to write their stories, taking a leaf out of the book of these female writers. Through the poetry, we collaboratively explored the hidden strength and resilience of ordinary women, who have experienced broken dreams and broken marriages, broken bones and broken hearts.

Reading these poems inspired me to write my own, which I shared with the group the following week.

I rise and fall
You learn to get up with dignity
No matter how ungraceful the fall might have been

You learn to cover bruises on your heart with invisible bandages
Every time it gets that little bit easier
You learn there is no real differences between joy and pain
Both make you cry

The women developed their writing skills through personal stories. Through their writing, they opened the window to their souls, allowing me to look into their world and see through their eyes the conflicts they left behind, only to face further challenges of dislocated communities who seek asylum. No one leaves their beloved homeland just for the sake of it and to come to the unknown.

During the sessions, there was a lot of negative press against Muslims and an increase in Islamophobia; a peaceful religion mischaracterised and seen as a threat. The group would bring in articles to share and debate, on topics such as women's role in Islam. Sometimes certain viewpoints were challenged, and participants engaged in heated deliberations. Despite the contentious nature of some of our discussions, the essence of the sisterhood group was that it created a safe space for women to develop and contribute to their own learning. Members of the group supported, encouraged and inspired each other, and I value their friendship and kindness.

Our research led to new insights and demonstrates that not all knowledge can be found in books; ordinary people living ordinary lives hold some amazing knowledge that needs to be shared. Beyond producing individual writings, the school-based group produced a book on folklore herbal medicine as part of the 'Imagine' project. Folklore medicine is a fascinating mixture of fable, myths and religious and cultural beliefs, combined with herbs and spices, creating a strong concoction of home, family, roots and history that even today in modern Britain is used by many people as traditional ways of healing. The creation of the book relied on group participants sharing stories and family narratives. I was so impressed with how much knowledge there is in our communities that often goes untapped, resulting in the loss of a rich part of our heritage and culture.

Our writing groups did evoke emotions. As a researcher, you cannot detach yourself from others, 'stay outside looking in' and not share your own narrative of life and your inner emotions. The importance of researchers' own feelings are acknowledged by McLoughlin (2003), who argues that, 'increasingly it is recognised that the researcher's own emotions are a necessary part of the research enabling the researcher to enter into the participant's world and gain a deeper understanding of it' (p.74). I would argue that emotions heighten your senses; they amplify what one hears, sees and feels. Emotions give the researcher a better and a more honest insight into participants' everyday lived experiences, their journeys and their sacrifices; in the case of this research, insight into the barriers that the women faced.

The work of Hubbard et al (2001) is referenced by Emerald and Carpenter (2015), who argue that, 'Emotionally sensed knowledges are the subtle knowledges, not knowledge of the emotions, but knowledge sensed through or by emotion – when the researchers' emotional senses "gain insight and give meaning to their interpretations of the subject that they are investigating"' (p.748). When you spend a lot of time with the research participants, you cannot remain totally objective, as it is almost impossible to explore the lives of others at an arm's length and to be emotionally detached.

The future and hope

As the political climate changes rapidly, the girls who were involved in the research gave me hope as to what the future could be like. The following poems, written by one of the writing group participants, demonstrate this notion of hope.

My home is a place that I love most
Where the sun shines always with happiness
It's a place where I feel safe
It's a place where I feel alive
A home is a place to store your worries
A home is a place to let your hair down
A home is a place where there is no darkness

It is hard to describe the emotions on the girls' faces as they talked about their imagined futures, about the women they wanted to become one day and the world they wanted to live in. It was a privilege to share in their visions and aspirations for their futures. Through their writing, they opened up a window to their inner feelings and allowed me access to their imagined future worlds.

The new world
The sun shines bright
The world begins again
Dancing and playing in the air.
Having too much fun, days go fast
Time passes away
In the new world I can bring time back and start again
I stay forever 10
Silver stars twinkling hello
The golden moon reaches out to shake my hand,
The breeze calls my name and says make a wish
I wish I can fly on clouds and never come down.

These writing projects captured the emotional journeys of women and contributed a multiplicity of voices about a variety of female experiences to academic research. The projects gave women who are underrepresented in research the opportunity to tell their stories through writing and poetry. Being part of the writing groups gave me an insight into the lived experiences of different generations of women from different parts of the world and an opportunity to see into their emotional world.

FIFTEEN

What parents know: a call for realistic accounts of parenting young children

Tanya Evans, Abigail Hackett, Joanna Magagula and Steve Pool

> Mothers live in a universe that has not been accurately described. The right words have not been coined. Using habitual vocabulary sends us straight down the same old much-trodden paths. But there are other paths to which these footpaths do not lead. There are whole stretches of motherhood that no one has explored. (Stadlen, 2005, p.12)

At Clifton Park in Rotherham, there is a fantastic playground, including a sand play area. We often go to the sandpit. The children pull off their socks and shoes and play with the sand, and take turns on the fast slide that lands in a pile of sand. We parents sit on the wooden boardwalk next to the sandpit. We take our shoes off too, bury toes or run fingers through the sand as we chat. After a little while, the children will probably come to sit on the wooden boardwalk too, and we will eat our packed lunch. It is a beautiful spot – you can see the hillside of the park rising up behind the sandpit, and the children always seem happy here. It is also a little stressful because it is often quite busy, and we try to keep our eyes on our children as they play and we chat.

This vignette typifies the meetings that took place between us, a group of researchers and parents, during collaborative research over a number of years near Clifton Park in Rotherham. As part of our collaborative ethnography, we organised a series of family den-building events, with community partners, in order to think through how children learn and have experiences in places.[1] We aimed explicitly to draw across and value different kinds of knowledge about young children – professional practitioner knowledge, academic knowledge, and particularly the knowledges gained from everyday lived experiences of being parents and children.

These kinds of everyday knowledges about the 'what' and 'how' of parenting young children are rarely represented or valued in policy discourses, and therefore risk being overlooked in practical initiatives designed to help or support families with young children in communities. By foregrounding and valuing these everyday lived experiences of families and children, we hope to offer more realistic accounts of what it means to parent young children, which we think should inform policy and practice regarding how young children should be cared for and should participate in communities. In writing this chapter, we hope to contribute answers to the question: how can we re-imagine provision for parenting and families with young children in Rotherham through the knowledge that exists in these families and communities?

The quote at the beginning of this chapter is taken from a book called *What mothers do: Especially when it looks like nothing* (Stadlen, 2005) and the title of our chapter, 'What parents know' is a deliberate reference to Stadlen's work.[2] While the focus of Stadlen's book is mothers' early parenting experiences, the way in which she presents nuanced, messy accounts of the emotional work of parenting, drawing mostly on the words of parents themselves, resonates strongly for us.

Two key messages run through *What mothers do*: first, the need to honour the complexity and hard work of mothering; and second, the importance of what Stadlen calls 'circles of mothers', that is, mothers listening to and supporting one another, even when they have made different decisions about parenting. Without the united voices of mothers themselves being represented in debates about child rearing, Stadlen argues, 'motherly achievements go unseen' (p.17) and stories remain untold.

Who are we?

We are a group of parents and researchers. Between the four of us (Tanya, Abi, Jo and Steve), we have over 47 years of parenting experience and more than 27 years of research experience. While as a group of four, we cannot begin to claim to represent the diversity of parenting experiences, we do encompass a range of different experiences that may resonate for many parents. Between us, we have had children with close age gaps, juggling babies with small toddlers, and we have had children with large age gaps, doing the school run after a night of feeding. We have experienced pregnancies that took us by surprise and were not planned, and pregnancies that took longer to happen than we would like. We have been stay-at-home parents, surviving on small incomes, and working parents, struggling with competing demands and guilt. We have raised our children a stone's throw from where we grew up, and on a different continent from where we lived as children. Our children currently range from 1 year old to 23, and we have personally each spent many hours as parents with our own children at the kinds of family events we organised and studied during this research. Some of us have qualifications in research methods, though for all of us, learning through doing was how we acquired the skills of ethnographic research (as well as our parenting skills).

Abi, Jo and Tanya all had young children at the time of doing the research and, as parents, we ourselves used the children's centres discussed later. Although Steve's children were at school, he had been a stay-at-home dad when they were younger. Therefore, this lived experience of bringing our children to playgroups, family events and children's centres as parents ourselves was something the four of us shared. Sometimes our children came with us to the den-building events. This chapter is about the interaction between what we know as parents and what we observed as researchers when we investigated young children's learning.

The context of us coming together as a research team is as follows. Abi had already carried out research (including her doctorate) at a local children's centre in Rotherham, and Jo and Tanya had participated in her doctoral research. Following her doctorate, Abi had worked with Jo and Tanya on a small project to explore collaborative ethnographic research, during which we all collected visual data about our children's learning (Hackett, 2017). Therefore, the three of us had already begun working together on a collaborative research approach, which we were keen to explore further. Meanwhile, Steve had been involved in a series of community-based research projects in Rotherham, and was invited to work on this project as the project's artist (although in reality our roles were much more blurred).

We organised a series of four family den-building events, run over an eight-month period (November 2013–September 2014) in different community venues in Rotherham: a museum, a multi-use community space, a children's centre, and a playgroup in a community hall. Each time, the events were run in partnership with community partners (the museum service and the children's centre). At each event, Steve led a den-building activity for families with children aged under five years, while our community partners provided additional activities, including craft, dressing up, storytelling and music. At each event, ethnographic field notes and hand-held video footage were collected by Abi, Jo or Tanya. As a research team, the four of us also met three times to analyse the data together.

Building dens on the floor and making craft at tables

> Crafts – By far the most popular stand of the event. There were crowns, shields and general crafts to be made. All the children, age notwithstanding, made one or more of the items. A lot of the mothers were also engaged in arts and crafts with their children. Girls tended to spend a much longer time with the crafts as well.

> Castle – As mentioned above, there was a lot of excitement at first, when the first castle was put up, all the children had a turn running in and out … The children who had friends/siblings played with them a lot more as they could chase each other through them and play hide and seek.

(Field notes, Jo, 28 May 2014)

At each event, Steve led a large-scale den-building activity, in which he used large sheets of card, plastic ties and oil pastels to work with the children to construct dens. Our community partners at each event also organised table-based crafts, involving sticking and drawing. As the den building was often conceptualised as a 'castle', the table-based crafts also followed a castle theme, including making crowns, shields and swords. Most children took part in both playing in the dens, and in the table-based crafts, moving between the two as they wished.

Generally, playing in the dens involved the children running in and out of the structure, through child-sized doors, and peeking through child-sized windows. They frequently dressed up, wore cardboard crowns, and carried the cardboard swords and shields they had made at the craft table. The children tended to play with each other, and their play was characterised by movement in, around and through the den, while parents stayed outside the den.

In contrast, the activities at the craft tables, which included decorating crowns, shields and swords with stickers, glitter and feathers, seemed to require sitting at the table. Parents frequently sat on the chairs at the tables too, and assisted their children to copy the sample crowns and swords, by helping them to reach resources, to cut things out and to use the glue sticks.

Therefore, in summary, the den building seemed to produce play between children, often involving fast movement, whereas the craft table seemed to produce collaboration between parents and children, which usually involved staying still. The children needed more assistance to make the craft at the table, but also when the children were stationary, it was easier for the parents to interact with them.

Our observations

To explore this contrast between how children and families behaved and experienced the craft table compared to the den-building area, we want to view our observations through different lenses:

- the early years policy context;
- an anthropological critique of that policy context;
- our own lived experiences of parenting.

In doing so, we bring lived experiences of parenting children into dialogue with the policy context on how parents should be supported or encouraged to parent.

Children's centres and the early years policy context

In terms of young children's communication, the focus in UK government policy is firmly on spoken communication, increasing the number of words young children choose to use, and on encouraging adults, particularly parents, to spend more time talking one to one, face to face with their children (for example Hart and Risley, 2003; Field, 2010; Roulstone et al, 2011). The differential development of language and communication practices in young children from poorer and wealthier households is of great concern to policy makers. However, policy responses tend to adopt a deficit perspective, blaming poor parenting or home environment for the lack of words (for example Hart and Risley, 2003; Clarke, 2006; Field, 2010). Research taking a snapshot of 'home environments' has concluded that environment is a crucial factor in language development (Roulstone et al, 2011), leading to significant investment in recent years in funding younger children to start nursery earlier.

Children's centres, alongside the majority of early childhood support and intervention initiatives (in the UK at least), also place a strong emphasis on spoken communication (words not gestures) occurring between children and their significant adults, for example parents.

In addition, children's centres are tasked with preparing children for starting school, and encouraging families to take up the offer of free nursery hours for their children from the age of two years.

Anthropological perspectives on young children's language development

Avineri et al (2015) point out the culturally specific nature of many of the ways in which Western parents are advised by policy makers to communicate with their young children, such as baby talk and playing peekaboo. Blum (in Avineri et al, 2015) urges a focus on interactions rather than labelling (nouns), in her critique of what she calls 'wordism', that is, the assumption that language is made up of words, and that more words are better than fewer words. In addition, Blum points out: 'Anthropological research shows, in fact, that addressing the youngest children as conversational partners is extremely unusual in the world. These linguistic exchanges have no communicative function except to reward children with parents' approval for passing the test' (Avineri et al, 2015, p.75).

Heath's (1983) seminal longitudinal ethnography of young children's acquisition of language in two communities in the US provided in-depth insights into how language practices (such as storytelling, gossiping and playing) became differently meaningful for children in these two communities in their very early years. There is well-established critique within anthropology (Avineri et al, 2015), sociolinguistics (Snell, 2013) and education studies (Grainger, 2013), about the narrow and culturally specific assumptions about young children's communication lying behind early childhood policy documents. Despite this, parents themselves are rarely positioned by policy makers as having any expertise with regard to family communication. Rather, the emphasis tends to be on what is seen as parents' problematic lack of knowledge about these specific, normative, government-sanctioned ways of communicating with young children (for example Whitmarsh, 2011).

Policy rhetoric and lived experiences: what is it really like to parent a small child?

Traditions of 'scientific' knowledge about children have sought to influence mothering (in particular) practices for many centuries. Opening his book *Essay on nursing* in 1748, Cadogan wrote:

It is with great pleasure I see at last the Preservation of Children become the Care of Men of Sense. In my opinion, this Business has been too long fatally left to the management of Women, who cannot be supposed to have a proper Knowledge to fit them for the Task. (Hardyment, 2007, p.10)

Hardyment's book traces a long tradition of scientific knowledge seeking to inform parenting practices, from the 18th century onwards. While the specifics of the advice have varied widely, it is characterised by (both male and female) experts drawing on latest research and theories to influence parents' behaviour, rather than parents relying on others in their communities for guidance. In the last 150 years, in particular, this requirement to adopt specific kinds of parenting practices for specific childrearing outcomes became conceptualised as a public duty, producing 'good stock' for the future benefit of the country.

Churchill and Clarke (2009) point out that a belief that parenting practices can solve problems such as social exclusion is a common recurring and increasing feature of UK policy. Initiatives such as SureStart and the children's centres have, from the beginning, focused specifically on 'at risk' parents, and coupled services for children with initiatives designed to influence the behaviour of parents, such as breastfeeding and smoking cessation. The emphasis on children's centres influencing how parents interact with, talk to or play with their children comes from this context. Working across our analysis of government policy rhetoric and anthropological literature, we are aware of the ways in which government policies frame the interactions that children's centres have with families (Clarke, 2006), as well as the history of political ideology behind some of these framings (Gillies, 2007).

Our own experiences of using children's centres concur with this wider literature. Such organisations offer valuable support to families and children, but through tightly framed models of what good parenting and childhood look like, which tend to limit the scope for parents to feel a sense of autonomy or expertise in their own parenting practices. For example, a notable characteristic of visiting playgroups run by children's centres (in our experience) is that staff emphasise interaction between parents and children. We each have personal experience of this. For example, we remember a display on the wall of a playgroup we used to attend, explicitly telling parents to read to their children, play on the floor with them and talk one to one with them for a certain number of minutes each day. When children played at the playgroup, parents were encouraged to play with them on the floor, rather than sit on chairs at the side of the room. Periodically, the chairs around the edge of the room in which the playgroup took place would be turned towards the wall, to discourage sitting down. Once, a parent fell asleep on the sofa during playgroup; staff regarded this as a failing in their mission to promote parent–child interaction, and the sofa was removed from the room.

But what is it really like to spend 24 hours a day with a small child and, as part of that day, to attend a playgroup and be so tired that you fall asleep on a sofa? Stadlen (2005) would argue that we lack the vocabulary to even begin to answer this question, and this is at the root of the problem with how parenting young children is conceptualised in society. Perhaps more collaborative research with parents will help us to find more language to talk about how this crushing kind of tiredness, which can build up over months or years, feels. Or language to explain the constant sense of distraction that comes with keeping children safe in public places, or the overwhelming sense of both powerlessness and intense responsibility one can feel in watching a child grow seemingly increasingly independent of you, while still being entirely dependent.

In addition, we would add that some of the answers to the question 'What is it really like to parent a small child?' cannot be articulated in words. This is something that we came to appreciate through doing research on this project, while also having young children ourselves. The ache through your arms from pushing a pushchair up a hill; the automatic jutting out of a hip to support a small child in your arms; the constant slight tension of adrenaline and flickering eyeballs that comes from keeping an eye on your child playing in the sandpit, while maintaining friendly conversation with other grown-ups. We can try to articulate these things in this chapter, but some aspects of experience can only be known from the inside (Ingold, 2013).

Viewed through the lens of enacting a policy of increasing parent–child interaction through engagement with the children's centre, we can see the rationale for removing the sofa from the playgroup. Viewed through our own lived experiences of parenting – involving a combination of years of broken nights, co-sleeping, night-time feeding and soothing, sleepless nights with sick children and staying up late to complete household chores, work and study once children are in bed – the act of removing the sofa seems almost brutal.

We write this analysis of the sofa hesitantly, because it is not intended as a criticism of one particular decision. Rather, we contrast the logic of the decision from the point of view of enacting a policy (intended to benefit families and to improve children's life chances) with the illogical nature of the decision from the point of view of lived experiences of parenting. This powerfully introduces the two competing lenses we worked across as parents and as researchers in this study. This disjuncture mirrors two visions for thinking about how children communicate and participate with their parents and wider communities – one is instrumental, tidy, measured and owned by policy discourses; the other is messier, more chaotic and yet, to us, more real.

Rethinking what parents know and do: sitting in the park

Towards the end of our research project, the four of us met in Clifton Park sandpit to talk about the project. Our children played together, while we sat, toes buried in the sand, talking. This mirrored the play that took place around the cardboard dens; play between children while adults sat back, characterised by moving bodies, interactions with place and materials, and children's non-verbal absorption in what they were doing.

We talked about how comfortable we felt allowing our children to play in this way, and how artificial intensive play interactions between adults and children can sometimes feel. We talked about our belief that when children get bored, it can fuel their creativity. We talked about the importance of letting go of control and of the need to understand the rationale behind what children do (Rautio, 2014). We talked about multiplicity; everyone has different ideas about how to raise children and, by doing something different, it is important parents do not feel they are doing something wrong (Stadlen, 2005). We talked about adult fear and anxiety; fear that children will get bored leads you to over plan (both as parents and practitioners - during our planning of the den building activities, we felt we were constantly resisting an urge to over plan). Related to this is adults' fear that only by increasing policy interventions and intensification of parenting (Gillies, 2007) can the proper development of young children be guaranteed.

These notions of fear and risk regarding children's development are pertinent to the discourse that shaped the children's play in the dens and at the craft tables during our study. As Ochs and Kremer-Sadlik (in Avineri et al, 2015, p.73) have argued, advice given to parents on how to talk to and spend time with their children 'rests upon a class-based and anxiety-filled vernacular notion of the child as a communicative (cognitive developmental) project'. Clarke (2006) points out that policies calling for an intensification of parenting risk parenting being seen as purely 'an activity whose purpose is to deliver children with the desired characteristics' (p.717). Sitting in the park with our children, we talked about the need for more realistic views of what relationships between parents and children look like, and the need for broader parameters within which parents could be judged as fulfilling their role in a reasonable way.

Through doing this research, as both parents and researchers, and drawing on both these ways of knowing in our thinking and analysis, we felt able to make sense of our own lived experiences of parenting in new ways. Specifically, we viewed our personal embodied experiences of both parenting and using children's centres through the policy and dominant research framings within which these things operate.

Who has the expertise on our children?

> Motherly achievements often go unseen. If there aren't words for them, how can we recognise them? (Stadlen, 2005, p.17)

We wanted to articulate the ideas in this chapter, not to critique parents or practitioners, but to argue for the importance of decentring official or academic expertise, particularly regarding a topic as personal, intimate and idiosyncratic as young children and parenting, and instead foregrounding the lived, experiential knowledge of parents themselves. When this happens, the jutaxposition between inflexible official advice and recommendations, and the subjectivity and multiplicity of parenting experiences, shows up in sharp relief. We want to articulate this because:

> Loads of parents are thinking and knowing this, and having this experience, but when they get into schools, there is no way of them saying this, they are made to feel like bad parents. So if not through research, how else can this be recognised? (Steve, group discussion, October 2014)

Researchers in the field of childhood are asked to provide knowledge in writing about what is best for young children and recommendations for parenting that can be generalised and universally applied. As parents using children's centres, we are aware of the alienating effect that such rigid and objective forms of knowledge can create:

> That is so true – when we first came to the Children's Centre you are made to feel like you should listen to the professionals. But through this research, you realise that you

are the expert, you know your own children. (Jo, group discussion, October 2014)

As parents, we draw on our lived experience of parenting, which is inherently subjective, flawed, contradictory and inconsistent, to say that relationships between parents and children take lots of different forms. As a result, we are calling for, firstly, a more authentic, complex, nuanced account of what it means to parent young children. Collaborative ethnography with parents offers the potential, we argue, to develop research methods that not only foreground lived experiential knowledge of parenting, but also make these embodied, tacit lived ways of knowing indivisible from research observations.

What would early years policy look like, we wonder, if as a starting point it considered deeply what is possible, realistic, authentic or even desirable regarding the ways in which young children and the adults who love them muddle through life together? We call for these things because when policies to support families and children take the lived experience of parenting as a starting point, then interventions to support parents and families could be genuinely supportive and inclusive to all families.

Notes

[1] We would like to gratefully acknowledge the funding we received for this work through Community Arts Zone, an international research project funded by Canada's Social Sciences and Humanities Research Council.

[2] A point of difference between our research and Stadlen's book is that we use the term 'parents' and she uses the term 'mothers'. We acknowledge that both these terms are problematic. All families are different, and the role that different adults play in the lives of young children varies greatly. We refer in general in this chapter to the adults who are mostly at home with their children, dealing with the daily (and nightly) minutiae of caring for young children. In the case of our research team, the term 'parents' is appropriate; however, in other cases this may be carers, grandparents, siblings, and so on.

SIXTEEN

Where I come from and where I'm going to: exploring identity, hopes and futures with Roma girls in Rotherham

Deborah Bullivant

The 'I come from' project, one of the strands within the 'Imagine' project, set out to work with a group of Rotherham's young women, defined as Roma by their school and the communities around them.[1] The project aimed to explore their experiences and visions of an imagined future and their fused identities and shared sense of belonging, all of which would be interpreted and presented through images, textiles, song and poems.

As individual stories came together, shared traditions and connections across cultures began to emerge. Fragments of stories, folklores and experiences began to flow into rich tapestries of experience. Creative re-interpretations of tradition revealed the shifting cultures and experiences that were shaping and reshaping the lives of these young women – and did so from their own perspectives, rather than from the perspectives of outside 'experts'.

In the very midst of the project's creative activities, however, the Jay Report into child sexual exploitation was released (Jay, 2014), letting loose formerly suppressed fears and anxieties about the population growth and perceptions of Roma communities in parts of Rotherham, especially around the town centre. Immediately upon the report's release, Rotherham's once suppressed racial and cultural tensions came to the surface. Perspectives across the communities changed quickly and significantly, and the growing differences between ethnicities and cultures became the focus of both individual actions and media attention.

It was not the originally intended outcome of this research project to explore the impact of racial tensions within the Roma community. However, the young people participating in the research felt that tension, and it deeply affected the findings and issues that emerged throughout the project. The aftermath of the Jay Report had an inevitable impact on the young people of this community and on the way they saw themselves and their futures.

Beginnings of the project

At the beginning of this project, we set out to examine the use of writing across communities and its role in resilience, development, culture and identity. Our plans were to:

- introduce the group to research skills (questioning and interviewing techniques and further research methodologies);
- explore folklore, stories, traditions – meanings and how these were shared within the group's individual experiences;
- facilitate and support the young people to create their own research;
- provide the facilities, resources and support to enable artistic dissemination of their findings;
- undertake at least three exhibitions of the young people's work within their own communities and at recognised spaces, including The Hepworth Wakefield art gallery, Millennium Galleries and Rotherham gallery spaces;
- provide opportunities for the young people to experience and explore the University of Sheffield and to visit other sites, which would broaden their understanding and knowledge on research, literacy, artistic representation of research findings and story.

Our initial plan was to recruit, through existing contacts with Roma heritage families, a group of between six and ten young women, aged 11–12, who would be involved in a project that explored their own stories, heritage, language, identity and positive aspects of their community and history.[2] We utilised a collaborative, participatory research approach (Lawless, 2000) and began by building a foundation of stories, heritage, arts and language that were familiar to all, while encouraging the participating young women to take this project where they thought it should go.

The project was initially proposed for six months, but it ended up running from early 2013 through to mid-2016. The secondary school with which we worked had a rapidly expanding population of children from Roma communities, many of whom were also transient. A regular group of 12–16 young women attended our Friday lunch sessions in their own time, bringing along their lunch and determining the agenda, methods and activities.[3] We began to explore the ground rules at the outset of the project. To do this, we were asked by the young women to explain what our aims were and what was expected of them. We stated that we hoped to explore and celebrate heritage and linguistic identities through the traditions, stories and experiences the young women would research, which they would illustrate with the help of artists.

The flip chart (see Figure 16.1) shows a mixed, shared and agreed upon idea of what participants could expect while writing stories. During the first session, the young women insisted – and the rest of us agreed – that the group had to 'have fun'. One young woman made a comment then that rang true throughout the project: 'Let me tell you, Miss – if you want it to be fun and exciting then you need to learn straight away that you can only do that with music and dancing where we're concerned'. This comment proved very telling about the participants and their home community. Music and dancing were the backdrop for all activities throughout the project, which the project's videos and photographs depict. The list also reveals that our goals were not likely to be achieved, if we set out to do all of our research and activities in a typical classroom environment.

Figure 16.1: What do you expect?   **Figure 16.2:** What do you expect of us?

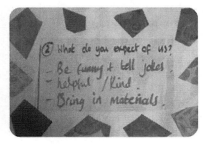

The second expectation flip chart (see Figure 16.2) asked, 'What do you expect of us?; 'us' being the adults/facilitators of the project. The key unanticipated surprise here was that we were expected to 'be funny and tell jokes'. At the outset, we had separately discussed how we might make this fun, and how it might develop the dynamic of the group in interesting ways if we were to be comedians at particular points in the process. So, each of the three supporting facilitators attempted to learn a new joke each week and approached the overall project with an attitude of allowing fun, having fun and embracing fun within the project. This led to a quickly developed respect and ease of interaction within the group. The young women enjoyed laughing at – and with

– the project facilitators, and they seemed to quickly become more comfortable in sharing their experiences and feelings.

Courage, respect and fun were the key features that underpinned the ground rules for this project (see Figure 16.3 and Figure 16.4), along with some additional, and again unexpected elements, like 'no sleeping' and 'turn up'.

Figure 16.3: What do you expect of yourselves?

Figure 16.4: What do you expect of each other?

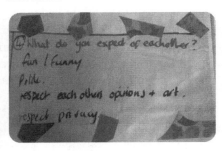

We then revisited the aims of the project, embedding the ground rules into the key aims and activities across the Friday afternoon sessions and into additional activities determined by the young women. Bearing this in mind, we set out to:

- equip the young people to determine appropriate methodologies, undertake research and disseminate the research using artistic approaches;
- explore traditions through story and its uses and influences across different communities;
- build the confidence of the young people to lead a research project within a given framework;
- provide space for reflection through writing, listening and speaking;
- engage families in the young people's project – as part of the research and in visiting the exhibitions/dissemination of the work;
- develop an understanding of literary art as a medium for communication;
- create artistic outputs, which would communicate the findings of the research undertaken by the young people.

The young women all agreed with this and stated that they were 'excited' to be involved in a project that would use art and research but 'wouldn't necessarily use the internet'. We – the project's adults and facilitators – were excited about being involved in a project that would expand their ideas about research, as well as their capacity to conduct it.

Exploring identity

In order to explore what they felt their imagined futures might be, the young women felt a need to rediscover their own individual identities. During initial meetings, discussions, drama activities and research activities, we explored the use of stories across the world and discussed stories that were familiar to the young people. We also explored art as a medium to communicate messages of hope and loss, or simply to inform and share an experience with others.

The young women identified the types of artists they would like to work with. The artists were to support them in an out-of-school day that would explore their individual identities and begin to use artistic methods to communicate their findings. I sourced a variety of artists: a creative writing tutor, a visual artist who wasn't afraid of pushing boundaries, and a textile artist with a traditional flair. All had to agree to adhere to the preset ground rules.

The young women also asked me to source lots of artistic resources (clay, textiles, cameras, various papers and pens, some transparent plastic, and other creative and craft resources), to provide the opportunity to explore their own identity. They also wanted me to find a local meeting venue, to speak directly to their parents to ensure that they would be allowed to come, and to provide food and drink.

The venue agreed by the group was a local youth centre, which was close to the school and used regularly by people from the Roma community, so would be familiar to their own families and not intimidating for the young women. Ethical permissions were given in full by the young people and their families for photos to be taken throughout the day and to be used in all media.

The topic of the day was 'I come from …'. The discussions were facilitated by the artists, but directed and led by the young women themselves, who then chose their own mediums to create their art and communicate their perceptions on their individual identities.

Figure 16.5 and Figure 16.6 show poems (transcribed below), reflecting the identity of the young women.

Figure 16.5: I come from

I come from my Rapunzel raven hair.
I come from my tidy ways.
Every morning I dance and my telephone is getting off.
Every day I make my mum annoyed because of my silliness.
My dad is laughing a lot because of what I do.
My Grandma and my Granddad are so good because they make me laugh.
Nigdy Nehova Nigdy. ['never say never' – Slovak]

I come from my brown/orange hat.
I come from my black/grey strong glasses.
I come from my old books, my playstation 2.
I come from my Jason Bieber singing.
I come from my spot bedroom.
I come from my bike fast car.
Nigdy Nehova Nigdy. ['never say never' – Slovak]

I come from graffiti on the paper

Figure 16.6: I come from hats

I wear lots of hats and I love cute cats.
I have my own swag but I am crazy when I wag my class.
I come from Hi-tops shoes when I moonwalk
I come from truth but I can't stop lying.
I come from the break in dance but sometimes I'm swearin'.
I come from gangs, come to us, we gonna give you a bang,
when you're down we gonna say slang, and we do our thang.
My heart is locked by a key!!

Embracing the fused nature of these young women's experiences, Barbara incorporated a traditional family saying into a traditional English cloth, because it materialised words that were important to her (Figure 16.7).

141

Figure 16.7: Barbara's image of a tapestry

Don't cry for love if it is lost. If it was love it will come back.

Figure 16.8: Simona's embroidery

While photographing the image in Figure 16.8, Simona explained that she had chosen this image to demonstrate the fusion of her current world. She positioned the objects she had created to show her words ('Smey Sa Teras Plac Potom' – partial translation: 'you laughed like a man can'), chosen to represent some words of meaning to her, stitched by her own hand onto what she felt represented a very traditionally English fabric. Her mobile phone, visible in the photograph's lower right hand corner, represented modernisation and change.

Another young woman chose to 'cover up' the words in her English textbook with a flamboyant statement of herself.

Figure 16.9: Writing on the book

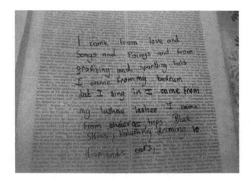

I come from love and songs and piercings from graffiti-ing and sparkling hats.
I come from my bedroom that I sing in.
I come from my luscious lashes.
I come from Shakira's hips, blue skies, halushkry dreaming to diamonds and cars.

Exploring hopes and futures

The young women collected their thoughts on aspirations, using postcards, flip charts and writing resources – thinking specifically about their thoughts on going to university – and created a collage of the outcomes, which they photographed. A telling phrase identified from cards the young women completed in response to the question 'What do you think of universities?' was: 'They are places for students and clever people, not like us!'

Further exploration of their perceptions of university led them to decide that they would like to go on a trip to see a university and to share some information about themselves with academics there. This was arranged by the project facilitators with support from the University of Sheffield. The young women were initially very nervous, but soon found their feet and enjoyed meeting the academics and discussing their exhibition, followed by a tour of the university with an enthusiastic doctoral student, who raced them around the areas of the building.

We asked the young women what they thought about the university and the academics who work and study there. One young woman said that she thought it was like a mini city but it had modern parts and historic parts, which made it an exciting and interesting building. Another young woman said that she had not thought she would be able to speak to academics, because she did not think that they would understand her, and she had thought that she probably wouldn't understand them either. She added that she was 'shocked' that some of the academics seemed just like her. She also stated that she had never imagined herself eventually going to university but, after this, she could really see it as a possibility. Another young woman agreed, stating that she thought it was an exciting place to be, and it had made her think differently about university as a possible place for her.

A group identity started to form among the young women. As a result of the teamwork that created the exhibition, the trip, and the joined-up thinking that was taking place, two of the young women put it to the group that they would like to create a 'name for the group', providing a team identity for others to see. They felt it should reflect the fact that they were female, but also that they were working as researchers on this project and were, in fact, academics in the making. Therefore, their discussion led to the creation of the identity 'Clifton University Girls', and one of the young women offered to create some samples of logos (see Figure 16.10), which she would bring in for a decision.

This revelation about possibilities in their futures that were other than those they had originally imagined led the group to begin thinking about how they saw their possible futures and what made them think that these were right for them as individuals.

Artists were gathered for further developments over two full-day workshops in the school holidays. This included the creation of a book box, which would represent: the biography of their imagined futures; representations of women, strength and barriers; their imagined homes; and, of course, music and dance. These 'book-boxes' (Figure 16.11–16.4) represent how the young women imagined themselves and their futures.

Figure 16.10: Clifton Girls logo

Figure 16.11: Nurse book

L's book: 'My book represents my caring nature – it is about working in a hospital and also having my own family. People would describe me as a caring person and I think I will use this in my imagined future to help others.'

Figure 16.12: Locked book

Figure 16.13: Fashion book

R's book: 'My book has many secrets – it is all about love and my heart and I would like to keep it to myself so I will keep it closed.'

S's book: 'I am always looking at fashion and it has been really important to me all my life. My mother likes to sew and back in Slovakia she was employed by lots of people to create beautiful dresses but here she can't do it any more because people don't know that she can. I would like to be one of the best designers in the world so that people call actual dresses and shoes by my name.'

Figure 16:14 Food book

V's book: 'I adore cooking and I really love colour – so I am planning to be a brilliant cook and have my own restaurant where I serve my own creations. People will come from everywhere to try my food.'

The impact of the Jay Report

The young women were aware of the Jay Report and that abuse of children had taken place. They had also experienced the arrival of helicopters circling overhead, but their lack of engagement with the media led them to believe they were police or authorities looking for 'bad people,' rather than media helicopters, a phenomena that speaks to their experiences in Eastern Europe. They stated that since the arrival of the helicopters their personal experiences of racist behaviour had increased.

We explored how this might affect their thoughts on their futures. Some said they would probably go back to their countries of origin, but that they would like to remain in the UK to go to college and work here. Others said they would be likely to stay in the UK, but would move around to other areas where parts of their family had settled, and which they perceived to be safer.

The following week, L brought in a rap that she had written following our discussions on racism and the future, and through questioning with A about a racist incident that she had described. L didn't want to read it out loud in front of us, but would record herself saying it on a talking postcard at home. The rap talked about how racism was ridiculous, because we're all the same colour in the dark.

Bully rap

You know what I found really funny,
You telling me to jump out of a window, and to drink bleach.
I'm not stupid enough to do it.
Being racist by calling us the 'n' word.
But guess what – everyone is the same colour skin
when the lights are off.
Threatening me to die, dude.
I have something to live for but you don't.
Are you jealous that I can speak more than two different languages?
I think you should open your eyes and study hard,
you think you're tough right?
I laugh when you act so tough dude.
My Grandma can beat you up,
Did You ever look in history dude?
I guess not because you
need to study hard and remember –
I'm not stupid enough to do everything you say.

The group were moved; they appreciated what L had done here, by turning the incident into research and then into a rap, to disseminate to others the stories of what was happening in her world and in the lives of those within her community (see Figure 16.15).

Figure 16.15: Research journal rap

We discussed how writing might be used as a tool for resilience – how L had used her diary entries and question notes to inform a poem that could be performed with music. L stated that she had found the experience rewarding, as it meant that something negative could be turned into something positive and could also be shared with others, to try to prevent it happening again and to send out the message.

On being asked whether racism had got better or worse, they said definitely not better. J suggested that it wasn't quite as bad when they were at primary school. When asked whether they thought it might get better in the future, A was quick to say no. She didn't think it would ever get better – 'It's part of being a human'. She talked about how even animals do it. She told us that she had two fish, and one of them tried to eat the other; and when her uncle chose his dog, the other dogs were all playing and his was sat on its own in the corner.

L said that from now on she was going to study really hard and to write more raps – one of them about racism. Here is another of L's raps:

I should make history
I'm like a mystery,
hated by jealousy
cause they envy me,
run up to my enemies
see if they remember me,
soon as they remember me,
I wipe away their memory.

Conclusion: exploring hopes and futures through research

From beginning to end, this project worked as a collaboration with the young women. They determined the aims, the direction of travel, the methods utilised, the people who would be brought in to support them, the research itself and the creative outputs.

At the beginning of the project, the young women were mainly pleased to be working on something 'different' and were a little perplexed by the idea of themselves as researchers, as they did not see this as a role that fitted with their identity. There was a scepticism about the whole project, and it was apparent from the beginning that trust would need to be earned from the facilitator and the assistants working alongside.

Some key methods used to build trust included:

- ensuring consistency at all times;
- honouring the ground rules set by the group (including telling a joke at the beginning of each session);
- ensuring that the young people's ideas and direction were valued throughout – all the way through the project to this dissemination.

As we researched and wrote together, the young women began to feel a sense of ownership with the group, and eventually began to think of themselves as researchers. The moment that demonstrated how much self-perceptions had shifted from the initial stages when they had laughed at the facilitator informing them that they would be the researchers, was when they chose their name, 'Clifton University Girls'!

This participatory community research project was a journey that took many paths, all directed by the young people as they were discovering their own preferred sense of direction. They used this project to test out approaches that would work for them, while exploring the world of research and their place in it. Their autobiographical enquiries looked inwards at personal experiences and at those of their closest friends, then presented their findings of hopes, identities and futures through artistic means.

The project itself became a journey of self-discovery through troubling times, exploring their own reactions and experiences within a community experiencing great disturbance. The young people stated that they felt empowered and valued by the university community and facilitators. The facilitators observed the capacity of young people being increased, and a 'can do' attitude being formed, while the body of knowledge was being created.

A wealth of deep knowledge sits within the communities we study. When we collaborate with those who possess that knowledge – to explore, interpret and present it together – unexpected outcomes will occur and our studies will be so much richer for it.[4]

Acknowledgement
With thanks to Laura Jenova for all her support for this project.

Notes

[1] 'Roma' is a term used to identify immigrant groups, mostly from the central and eastern European countries. The term 'Roma', first chosen at the inaugural World Romani Congress held in London in 1971, is now widely accepted across the European Union as a generic and pragmatic term to describe a diverse range of communities, tribes and clans. Source: https://newint.org/blog/2013/10/28/roma-minority-prejudice.

[2] I, Deborah Bullivant, Director of Grimm & Co (a literacy charity, based in Rotherham), coordinated and facilitated the project along with assistant research support from Sophie Turner (Volunteer Coordinator at Grimm & Co) and, initially, with research student Eirian Burke.

[3] Permissions have been given for photographs and names to be used throughout this chapter. However, to protect name identities, we have chosen to keep the names of the young women anonymous within the text.

[4] Thank you to: the Clifton University Girls; Sophie Turner (Research Assistant); Laura Jenova; the school; Lenka Purshouse (TA and interpreter); the University of Sheffield; and all the volunteers who supported this project.

SEVENTEEN

Introduction to artistic methods for understanding contested communities

Kate Pahl and Steve Pool with Marcus Hurcombe

Art includes a huge diversity of practice and a commitment to knowing together and making together. In this book, we profile the work of individual poets and we showcase work by young people in poetry and visual images. We also articulate an approach to knowing through art, in that we recognise the need for artists as individuals to intervene and change the world. The process of making involves a process of change.

In our previous research on artists and what they did, we called this aspect of making art the artist's 'ego' (Pahl et al, 2017). Cassie Limb (see Chapter Twenty) can call up her experiential knowledge of form and shape to explore a sensory vision of the world with the girls she worked with. Zahir Rafiq's vision of the portraits (see Chapter Eighteen) comes partly from his own skill and experience, but is also visionary.

Making art can be a wrought process, a skill that is honed over time, such as the poems, but it is also fresh, anew. The poetry and the images in this book call up experience that is complex, entwined with place, but also wrought through complex experience that maybe does not reach mainstream media. Experience is also captured through art. In Shahin Shah's chapter (see Chapter Seven) it is possible to visualise some of the oral stories told by older South Asian community members – the vivid colours; the artistic lens enhances what has been told. Artists refresh and bring to life stories through images, often 'saying what has been unsaid' by the oral storyteller.

Working with artists sometimes means changing gear, and recognising different perceptions of the world. It might mean seeing things through the lens of the material, the situated, or the embodied, surfacing 'material knowledge' in Paul Carter's words (2004). Art as knowing can be developed through conversations, walks, in moments of interaction that create spaces for more things to happen. Art is a process, and here we think about how things emerge – stuff comes from stuff: trying, helping, working, making, talking – new ideas come from doing.[1] By this, we mean that as we created this book, and the artworks were developed, we learned from each other, and listened to each other's stories.

Many of the artistic pieces in Part Three were generated through conversations. Grant Kester (2004) wrote about the ways in which artists can create 'empancipatory insights through dialogue' (p.69). The insights of artists such as Zahir Rafiq helped us to think differently about the everyday lived experiences of British Muslims in Rotherham. Cassie Limb's work re-situated the thinking of young girls of Pakistani heritage in Rotherham and helped them to imagine better communities. Shahin Shah (see Chapter Seven) re-visioned the experience of Pakistani girls and women in Rotherham to create hopeful visions of the future.

Autobiographical writing is a way of articulating hidden voices. Poetry offers an emancipatory lens for thinking about identity and frees up young people to articulate differently their hopes and fears. Ryan Bramley and Ray Hearne's poems (see Chapter Five) evoke a post-industrial Rotherham – one of steel and deep-lived experience of industrialisation. In the photographic images, young people offer a gentle, lived version of Rotherham. All these visions are possible though art. Art enables us not only to see things in different ways, but also to see them from different perspectives.

Artistic approaches to knowledge include uncertainty and can be disorientating. In a previous research project,[2] Steve Pool, Kate Pahl and colleagues explored, through interviews and detailed research, what artists did when they worked with communities, and tried to find out some of the essential attributes that could be associated with artistic practice (Pahl et al, 2017). We discovered that artists were often able to produce artwork in response to community concerns, and to help people express themselves. They provided an attention to process, a focus on conversations and a need to stay in a space of uncertainty, difference and disorientation. It is important to include both kinds of artistic practice – that which is visible (poetry, visual art, sculpture, drawing) and that which is more of an approach, an orientation, a way of working and a commitment to openness and possibility.

Knowledge that is produced through art can be different. It is less linguistically focused, and more experiential and visual. While demographic information, surveys and interviews provide one kind of knowledge, arts methods provide insights into lived experience. The chapters in this book focus on images, poems and new insights. They involved doing things that might be unexpected, might lead to different kinds of insights from social scientific understandings that are linguistically located. Material knowledge, that rests on the senses, on visual and gestural experience, is differently weighted. The arts can open up voices to people who otherwise do not get heard.

Conversations between people lead to understanding, and art forms such as poetry present a powerful picture of life, that social science statistics cannot reach. As an example of this, youth worker Marcus Hurcombe describes a workshop involving a pebble and a story.

Holding the pebble

'Carve what you know as truth on stone and what you do not know, cast upon the waters' (old family saying).

During a windswept and blustery day on a Brighton beach, Kate Pahl and I (Marcus) gathered pebbles of many shapes, forms and textures to the thunderous roar of waves crashing upon the shore. Our purpose wherein was to deliver a break-out session to a group of academics and community partners, to highlight how the use of simple objects can gather truth and co-create meaning. With the chairs laid out in the round, I poured the bag of pebbles in the centre of the room, forming a cairn, thus beginning the process of connecting the outside natural world, with the created space.

In turn, each participant was asked to select a pebble that they felt had some attraction, be it colour, shape or texture. On holding their chosen pebbles, with tentative trust gained, they were asked to examine the pebbles closely, then close their eyes, feel, then sense the illusive connection, reach in and form a bridge from the outer to the inner emotive worlds: 'As you hold on to your special pebbles you are safe, relaxed, warm and protected from the outside elements'.

At this point, the outside elemental conditions are a metaphor for the turmoils and tribulations of life, whose multifaceted natures may perhaps remind us of life before the first handprints appeared in caves.

With the room now in silent contemplation, the group slowly opened their eyes and were asked to retrieve a word or emotion from their inner selves. Once released, these were collated into a piece of prose and read back, thus capturing and co-creating a vignette of the unconscious selves within a shared group experience.

In this vignette, shared collective knowledge is released through tactile and sensory experiences. Art can involve a product, but it is also a process. In thinking about art, bear in mind the process of creating art. The work also creates new ideas. Zahir Rafiq in his portraiture project helps us, as viewers, to think differently through his explanations of his portraits, but also, we learn through the depth of his visual imagination. Art is about finding shared histories together. Zanib Rasool wrote to me (co-editor of this book), in private correspondence, that:

> knowledge of past histories of migration and travel is captured through art, the lived experience of those who left their homeland to come to this country, our parents' sacrifices, my mother's isolation and loneliness, not being able to speak English and having no friends. My father's hard toil working long hours in a steel factory for little pay to feed his family in a harsh cold environment, working towards a better life. This is real lived knowledge that is captured through the process of doing art.

In this book, art is doing things. It is creating new visions for the future for the girls in Rotherham. It is making a space for a visual artist to paint strong portraits of women. It creates opportunities for girls to write about who they are. It speaks to the pain of the steelworkers and the coal miners who made this town. We celebrate the way in which art can tell us about community, but also art can shape and reflect community. Art can create a space to say things that can't be said. In the arts, things can be surfaced that do not fall into familiar patterns.

Art practice is a potential space. It is linked to a kind of unknowing, where the world stills and we think again, and reflect again, and out of that nothing comes something. Amanda Ravetz writes about ways of knowing that draw on tacit and felt knowledge, are intuitive, and can be a powerful enabler for solving complex problems (Ravetz and Ravetz, 2016). Unconscious, experiential and intersubjective thinking is hard to quantify but essential to ways of knowing that surface new insights and holistic forms of knowledge that take in a wide view of the world.

Art as it is today concerns itself with the intimate details of life, but often sits on the edge of life. Current trends and a move towards participation, coupled with the idea of life as form, brings art away from the rarefied exploration of the transcendental and sublime into the everyday. Art is not an ecology or a continuum; art is in conflict with itself and the world, a stepping into and a leap away. People can look to the idea of art for many things and art can hold these ideas for a moment or a glimpse, but by its nature it is fleeting. Art can do something to help us understand the in-between spaces better, the 'slant' spaces we need to open the door on and let breathe.

Art is a connective, a weaving process, and in the making of stuff, identities are inscribed. Art can connect family histories, create a sense of being between generations of the same family, 'my mother's story told in a different way' (Zanib Rasool). It opens up new opportunities for children to learn about their own history and heritage, which is otherwise slowly being erased. Artistic knowledge is located in images, poems and ideas, but also calls up past experiences.

Through art, visual images and poetry, the writers and artists in this book wanted to celebrate the lives of their parents and their generation, for giving them the opportunities that were denied to their parents' generation. 'We have not forgotten the sacrifices you made for us' (Zanib Rasool). It is a way of remembering them. These chapters sing out about ways of knowing that are themselves unknown and yet to be discovered. By placing artistic knowledge in the mix, we can hear communities differently, but we also become different in the process.

Notes

[1] From 'The Manifesto' by The Polytechnic: www.poly-technic.co.uk.
[2] Co-producing Legacy: What is the role of artists on Connected Communities projects (funded by the Arts and Humanities Research Council).

EIGHTEEN

What can art do? Artistic approaches to community experiences

Zahir Rafiq in conversation with Kate Pahl and Steve Pool

This chapter draws on a conversation held in Rotherham central library café between Kate Pahl, Zahir Rafiq and Steve Pool. All of the quotations from Zahir in this chapter come from the transcript of this conversation. We explore with artist Zahir Rafiq his lived experience of Rotherham, and how he has used art to create a space for conversations and for the articulation of experience. In doing so, we ask the question, 'What can art do?' and in this process, we argue for the arts as a mode of enquiry as well as an articulation of experience:

> I belong to a generation that were pushed and pulled from our cultures and our generation, feeling excited and exploited by all these things. (Zahir interview, 22 July 2016)[1]

Zahir Rafiq is an artist whose work has tried to probe and interrogate contemporary images and perceptions of British Muslims. At the same time, Zahir has worked primarily as an artist, someone who goes beyond the stereotypes assigned to him by the media or community descriptions. He has used his art to create positive images of British Muslims and to work closely with the police, faith organisations, schools and universities to develop contemporary images of the people and experiences he sees around him. Zahir's realisation in his work was that in order to convey everyday experience, art provides a way to sidestep many difficulties. Working as an artist provides an opportunity to be a different kind of social commentator. Zahir's story illustrates how art can become a way of articulating community experiences in a different way.

Zahir grew up in Rotherham, and his work draws on the twin traditions of Islamic art and Western artistic practice. Both Zahir's great-grandfather and grandfather were mosque builders. This involved both designing, building and decorating mosques, and was a skilled activity. Being a mosque builder involved designing and making the mosque and decorating the mosque with Islamic calligraphy. While this was not seen as 'artistic', it was part of a tradition where people decorated and inscribed images as part of everyday practice. When a mosque was completed, the community had a party to celebrate. When Zahir's grandfather came to England, he then got a job in a cutlery factory – making spoons. Zahir's mother was a skilled needlewoman and for thirty years was a dressmaker. Zahir reflected on how art was associated with making and skill in his family:

> Art was just a skill [in the context of the mosque building] – it was just thought of as a trade, but not something people would talk about in families ... engineers and doctors it was like 'my son's an artist' they [his family] can't comprehend that.

Being an artist, but also a social commentator and visionary, is something Zahir has developed over the years. He has remained true to his roots, but has always moved his work on to reflect the changing communities around him. Zahir's vision was to unite his identity as a Yorkshireman, rooted in Rotherham, bringing up a family, and trying to develop a specific way of being that combined his twin identity:

> I want to get to something that is Yorkshire Islamic art, something different, something new, with this project you have got to take risks and if you don't take risks nothing changes.

Zahir was concerned that engaging with communities often fell into familiar channels. For example, when consulting with the British Muslim community, people would often go to (often male) community leaders, but not to young people, women, or people who did not engage with meetings and structures. Young people, and their experiences and cultures, were often caught between two worlds and misunderstood in trying to articulate new identities. These new identities were sometimes lost in this process of consultation. When the 'familiar' people were consulted (for example faith leaders and community representatives), young people often felt left out and underrepresented. In Zahir's work, there was a focus on creating changes in people's perceptions of the British Muslim community as well as a focus on new voices. One of his earliest exhibitions was in a church as part of a 'Faith to faith' exhibition, which took place in 2002, just after the events of September 2001. He describes this in his own words:

> As a contemporary British Islamic artist my main aim was to use my art as [a] vehicle to create understanding and awareness about my Muslim faith. By exhibiting my artwork in a conventional setting such as a gallery I questioned myself, was this achieving the desired impact of bringing different communities together? I felt I needed to do something unique that would create more of an impression, something that had an element of risk. So, I embarked on organising an exhibition of Islamic artwork in a church, which to my mind it was probably the first of its kind. In August 2001 I contacted the Rotherham Churches Tourism Initiative. They were enthusiastic about the idea and we quickly gained support from the Vicar and the Bishop of Sheffield, which gave us both the confidence to push ahead with the exhibition. Neither of us could have foreseen that the events of September 11th of that year would add greater significance to the exhibition.
>
> At this time I had second thoughts of going ahead with the exhibition, I felt a sense of hopelessness and doubts about the exhibition having any effectiveness to bring people together in a time where communities seemed fractured. A number of factors refocused me on going ahead with [the] exhibition. The first was my baby daughter; as a father I didn't want her to grow up in an atmosphere that stigmatised her for the colour of her skin or her beliefs. The second was the support from my family and friends. The Vicar personally felt that the exhibition would be a change for the good and an ideal situation for creating community cohesion. With this encouragement on October 15th 2001 we staged the ground breaking exhibition of Islamic Art displayed in a Church. The event was called 'Faith to Faith'. The exhibition generated an overwhelmingly positive reaction from the general public. Muslims who had never stepped into a church viewed the exhibition and it provided Non-Muslims [with] an insight into the commonalities between Christianity and Islam and nurtured a new appreciation for Islamic art.
>
> Word spread of this unique event, so much so that I appeared in a national exhibition for Islamic Awareness

Week in 2004. The theme of 'Your Muslim neighbour' … sought to highlight the valuable contributions made by Muslims from all walks of life to British society.

For me the exhibition was a great example [of] how art can bring people together to promote community cohesion. In a small town like Rotherham an exhibition such as this can be organised with little resources and the success was down to the will of the participants who contributed their time and believed in this venture [. It] turned out to be a beacon of hope in a turbulent time. Of all the projects and exhibitions I have personally been involved in since then, I hope that The Faith to Faith exhibition will be seen as the birth of my artistic legacy.

Zahir's work on the 'Faith to faith' project led to further work in the community. This included being asked by South Yorkshire Police to design an 'Eid card' and an interfaith calender, to promote positive images of relations between the police and faith communities. One of Zahir's defining images is 'Hope Street' (see Figure 18.1), which is an image of a bicycle leaning against a mosque. This was produced as part the series of Eid cards commissioned by South Yorkshire Police in 2003-4.

… some police officers came up to me and said we would like to commission you to do an Eid card as we would like to get to grips with the issues and engage with the community and so forth. I jumped at it and then I thought what can I produce as an Eid card for South Yorkshire Police and with my art work I really wanted to find a vehicle of understanding to promote my faith and culture and identity …

That's when I thought, at that point when I had the police commission this is the ideal time to incorporate something I had been working on which is what is British Islamic art and how can I convey everyday, boring everyday, things that people see and everyone can relate to and how to put that into a piece of work. The best way I could do it was to find a balance between Islamic art and a normal street scene, a normal terrace, a street with a mosque there and people can relate to that more and that is what I designed for South Yorkshire Police. It was entitled Hope Street and the difficulty was how to incorporate elements of the police

– a vehicle would send the wrong message across, so I put a bicycle done digitally it was just represented as a normal street scene. The police said we appreciate this – using art and design to represent the community …

Figure 18.1: Hope Street

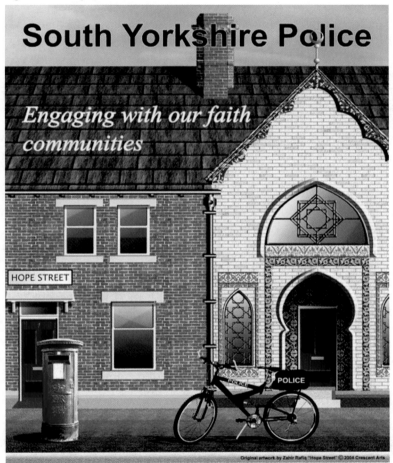

In this picture (see Figure 18.1), the bicycle becomes the everyday, the common culture, which is, as Zahir says, 'boring'. The mosque, likewise, is a normal terrace. Lived experience is thereby translated and constructed to create new ways of understanding communities, beyond media distortions that often portray Muslim communities as segregated and living apart from white communities (Robinson, 2008).

The everyday and common cultures: every object tells a story

At the core of Zahir's work is his persistent admiration for the everyday, lived experience of being a British Muslim. Beyond current concerns about racism and the contemporary fallout from the Brexit vote and community cohesion issues lies another world – of small-scale interactions and located experience, materially realised through objects, and linguistically realised through stories.

The 'Every object tells a story' project was a project that sought to find the common cultures in communities through stories and objects.[2] Kate Pahl, working with Zahir, had sought to identify ways in which families interacted in terms of objects and stories, and was interested in developing projects that listened to stories of migration and identity. Her project, 'Artifacts of migration and narratives of identity', was an attempt to capture some of these. Funded by the Arts and Humanities Research Council's Diasporas, Migration and Identities programme in 2006, the project enabled an exhibition, a website and a teaching resource pack to be produced. Zahir's contribution was to create a unique vision of the stories, together with the objects falling through space. The exhibition and website combined sensory appreciation of the power of gold together with an understanding of what brought people together – football, travel, weddings and everyday objects on mantelpieces (Pahl with Pollard and Rafiq, 2009; Pahl et al, 2009). These objects could speak with two voices, often multilingual, and had their own agency. The Singer sewing machine, found in many homes in Rotherham, united communities as a shared object, as it was clear that most households in Rotherham had one in the 1960s. Objects on mantelpieces, clocks and images of family success, were common to all. In the case of the 'Every object tells a story' project, Zahir's unique vision as an artist informed the project, as well as providing a way of representing objects, as falling through space and time, moving across from Pakistan to the UK and then being linked to communities and cultures.

Identity, culture, hope

Zahir's more recent project, now completed, was a set of portraits of British Muslims funded by the 'Imagine' project. Through this, he aimed to describe what being a British Muslim meant to him:

> The portrait project was my attempt to explore the changing attitudes of the British Muslim community, highlighting the transitions when some British Muslims became more secular in their outlook and their faith became a more peripheral part of their identity. I chose portrait painting as a medium to convey this concept because I feel that visual art provides better insight into this study of identity. Visual art can influence the opinion of people outside the Muslim community by providing them [with] a window into the opinions and views of British Muslims who have integrated into British society. As a British Muslim artist I strive to produce art that reflects my own British identity. I started out by incorporating traditional Islamic motifs into my work in an effort to predict the trends and tastes of British Muslims. My aim with this early work was to provide a different perspective on what can be developed into a new art form that can be classed as British Islamic art. I felt the only way forward for me as an artist was to paint portraiture.
>
> The key narrative behind these portraits was everyday lives, exploring identity and themes of how British Muslims see themselves and their place in society. How do they see their faith and what does their heritage mean to them? How do these things reconcile with their British nationality? Is it difficult to maintain a balance? Are they part of a community? I chose the medium of paint rather than photography as I felt it has greater power to draw the viewer into the picture. Each brush stroke has a story. The closer you look, the more you see. I felt the best way to make these portraits accessible was to strip away the labels altogether and just focus on the human beings behind the faith, to depict British Muslims of all walks of life, both traditional and progressive, with their hopes and dreams and contradictions, in situations that might not necessarily accord with orthodoxy of their faith.

Coming from a visual artist background taking on a researcher's role, I was not necessarily out of my depth because in the past I have had experience working on projects with academic partners where I had the opportunity to observe and gain an understanding of the concept of ethnographic research and how data was obtained from interviewing. I implemented an interview method, by organising an initial informal meeting to pitch the concept to potential participants about the project and then if they agreed, I would ask them to take part. With this body of work I hope I have achieved a way to provide an insight into British Muslim Identity and how their faith defines them, but also how they are the product of other influences, both external and internal. And I hope I have shown the change from a generational perspective of where the Muslim community was, where they are now and where they are going.

Six portraits explored

Zahir presents six portraits of British Muslims and describes what they mean to him.

When Zahir first started the project, his mother was still working in her material shop in Eastwood in Rotherham. She had built up this shop through her own energy and determination. She was proud of her shop, its bright fabrics and strong profile in the local community. People saw this as a hub for the community, and also Zahir's mother was part of the fabric of the community. Zahir saw the portrait (see Figure 18.2) as celebrating her achievements. Here he describes the work:

> The first portrait is of a First Generation immigrant named Mumtaz Begum, a composition depicting the subject standing before a wall of rolled exotic fabrics. She arrived in Britain in the 60s, eventually settling in Rotherham. She brought with her a keen interest in sewing. At the time it was difficult for Asian women to purchase traditional garments. So women like Mumtaz thrived by providing a service making handmade garments. Mumtaz became an astute business woman, running her own fabric and clothing business and becoming a shop owner. Mumtaz Begum also happens to be my mother.

For me this portrait is all about my mother's passion for fabric and a sense of pride in what she has achieved, her persistence in pursuing her passion, from modest means to founding her own business. From the earliest days, Asian women possessed an entrepreneur spirit and the freedom to follow their aspirations. The painting is also about expressions of textures from the rolls of material to my mother's head scarf and face and her coat. I wanted the painting to depict her surrounded by what she loves. The image also communicates the Knowledge that my mother has accumulated over the years about fabrics. The roles of fabric to me have the appearance of a shelf of books, and so I entitled this piece 'Material knowledge'.

Figure 18.2: Material knowledge

Zahir's focus for the initial portraits was on women who were strong, contemporary and stood up for their beliefs. Here he describes a portrait of a woman known as 'Tattooed Hijabi' (see Figure 18.3):

> From traditional, I moved to something more contemporary for my next portraiture. I found my next subject on social media. Her profile name was 'Tattooed Hijabi'. I emailed her and explained my project and I asked her permission to create a portrait based on one of her profile pictures. She happily agreed. The intriguing thing about her was that although in traditional Islamic dress, she wasn't covering her tattoos. They were part of her identity and a past she was proud of. She clearly stated on her social media profile that a person who converts to Islam or is born into the religion is on their personal journey of discovery. And she felt strongly that she wanted to express her Muslim identity through her contemporary fashion and to stand as an inspiration to other young Muslim women. This portrait depicts the confidence and freedom of expression in young Muslim women of today with their own styles; hijabi fashionistas if you will. Fashion is an excellent marker to show how a minority has integrated. I called this painting 'Marks of faith'. I feel that the portrait is the perfect partner piece to the portrait of my mother. Together they create a bridge from the past to the present.

Zahir wanted to celebrate young people and their achievements, from their own perspectives. His work celebrates a young man called Omar and his stance, head held high and with a positive perspective, who reflects those values (see Figure 18.4):

> This image is of a young man named Omar and it captures a pivotal moment in his life. This young man has just passed his degree and his whole future ahead of him. Education is a core value of Islam; knowledge enables you to grow and become connected to a wider world. These were the values instilled in Omar by his parents. Omar sees his faith as an integral part of his identity, even though he was born in the UK. Omar feels that the parameters set by Islam fit very easily into a western upbringing. I paint the face in profile to depict a young man facing his future. The piece is entitled 'I am Omar'.

Figure 18.3: Marks of faith

Figure 18.4: I am Omar

Zahir was also concerned to address images of British Muslim women as being powerful in their own right (see Figure 18.5 and Figure 18.6). He wanted to question people's assumptions about women within the Muslim community. He saw the women he painted as powerful and outspoken. In Zahir's words:

> My next two portraits are dedicated to the theme of empowered Muslim women. Shazana grew up as a shy child in a conservative, Muslim family. She wore a head scarf and nurtured a yearning to leave a mark in life. After her time in University she returned to Rotherham with emboldened confidence. Through her work as a youth worker she instilled this confidence in other young Muslim women who lacked confidence, some whom had endured difficult times with relationships and domestic abuse. Community issues in the Muslim community tend towards being dominated by male voices. Shazana has strived to ensure that her voice and the voices of other Muslim women are also heard. In the painting Shazana is seated in a pose that communicates self-assurance. This piece is entitled 'Confidence'.
>
> The next portrait in the empowerment diptych is of a woman named Sabrina, who was previously known as Shabina. Her name change served as a mark of her western integration. She is a professional bodybuilder, which is almost unheard of amongst Muslim women. This is her passion. She feels a conflict with her faith when competing. Her opinion is that fitness is a discipline and can be compared to the discipline required to keep faith. However, her fitness training is about her body image, whereas her faith is about her identity and about who she is on the inside.
>
> These two portraits depict modern Muslim women, not victims, not oppressed, but assured and in command of their own identity. On the surface there is nothing that readily identifies these women as Muslim. The revelation that they are of Islam puts them in a new light. The pictures are transformed in the eyes of the viewer, challenging preconceptions.

These women occupy the normal, common space of the everyday and the familiar, despite being unfamiliar in more conventional terms.

Figure 18.5: Confidence

Figure 18.6: Sabrina

Zahir's portraits were intended to start a conversation. They were there to create discussion and to provoke comments and, perhaps, to change perceptions. When describing his portrait of a man walking a dog (see Figure 18.7), he wanted to make this an interactive, thought-provoking piece of work:

> In the Muslim community, owning a dog is something that tends to be frowned upon as dogs are seen as unclean. Yet many Muslims do keep dogs as pets. Britain is a dog loving nation. What better way to communicate our common grounds than a picture of a man walking his dog in the park? Unlike the previous portraits which focussed on a single aspect of the subject, this picture tells a story, a visual narrative of a man with his dog in the outdoors. It is my intention to incorporate this theme of broader narrative in future pieces. The man in the painting is named Areeb, but my intention was to draw focus more to the dog. This portrait is entitled 'Bobbi'.

Figure 18.7: Bobbi

These portraits are, in a very specific way, trying to encourage the viewer to think differently about a community. The portraits are about changing perceptions as well as developing a vision of what communities could be. They unite a generalist vision of communities, with a particular, individual vision of where people are and where they are going.

Making sense of the world through art invokes a different way of understanding the world. In this chapter, we have provided a window on 'what could be', through the portraits. People are at ease, proud of their achievements and live within a culture of aspiration within the everyday. Often communities and lived experience are caught up in a discourse of failure – of things that have not happened and mistakes made – and more rarely personal discourses of success come through.

While the 'exceptional' is often lauded in sporting and media achievements, here is the exceptional in the everyday, the ability people have to make their lives positive through their lived experience. Zahir's contribution was to create a vision for communities and their futures that was refracted through the everyday and through the articulations of the everyday that were also exceptional. Art can celebrate the unusual as much as it can celebrate the ordinary. This conundrum shines through Zahir Rafiq's work.

Notes
[1]   All the interviews took place on 22 July 2016.
[2]   See: www.everyobjecttellsastory.org.uk.

NINETEEN

Using poetry to engage the voices of women and girls in research

Zanib Rasool

There is a growing interest in the use of creative or arts-based methods within social research. These are opening up spaces outside the boundaries of traditional methods of data gathering; a space that improves 'critical attentiveness, collaboration and experimentation' (Back and Puwar, 2012, p.18). Poetry as research methodology can elicit thoughts, feelings and emotions, and can give a platform for marginalised voices, such as women and girls, as it enables those silenced voices to be heard – and heard loudly.

During the 'Imagine' project, poetry was used as a research methodology by a group of women participating in a writing group at the community library. As a part of that group, I wrote the following poem, which exemplifies the emotions captured in poetry:

The voices of silent women
Tell me who is going to listen to those once silent voices?
Now Screaming to be heard
Invisible right before your eyes
The little girls who were neither seen nor heard
No longer wanting to be at the back of the queue
Ignore them at your own peril for they are demanding to be listened to
They have been gagged for far too long
Now it's their turn to speak the truth

A different lens to knowledge production

In the introduction to Part Three of this book (see Chapter Eleven), Elizabeth Campbell considers what kind of knowledge matters, and who should have a say in its production. As a community development worker and activist for over 30 years, my answer to that question is: the members of the communities whose lives are being investigated through research. They are the real experts on their own community and are responsible for producing the everyday knowledge in those diverse communities.

Poetry offers one way to capture the knowledge held in communities, particularly among those whose voices have been traditionally marginalised, like young people and women. Poetry provides us with a different lens for making sense of everyday interactions, contradictions and conflicts. Our cultural frame of reference – ethnicity, spirituality and faith, our interaction and experiences – means we see the world though different lenses. Poetry allows us to express those different perspectives of our lived experiences, a mosaic of autonomous voices freed through poetry.

bell hooks (1984), in her writing on feminist theory and feminist movement, says that for those on the fringes of society, '[p]oetry allows individuals to utilise their marginality' (p.2). She argues that: 'it is essential that Black women recognise the special vantage point our marginality gives us and make use of this perspective to criticize the dominant racist, classist, sexist hegemony and create a counter hegemony' (Hooks, 1984, p.2). Through poetry, women on the margins can challenge the existing status quo, give voice to women's political struggles and produce counter-narratives.

Poetry allows us access to the personal world of others and the opportunity to observe the everyday. Artistic approaches, such as drawings, paintings and writing, open a door to a different kind of conversation, a different way of knowing. Things are articulated through arts practices that otherwise may remain unsaid. For example, poetry gave me a historical contextual lens of growing up in Rotherham during different periods of my life. It also gave me an opportunity to have a nostalgic look at my own childhood, when the Rotherham steel industry was thriving and the sky was always grey from the smoke coming from the factory chimney towers, the long summer days of playing in the woods at the back of my street; poetry brought these memories of childhood back for me once again. Eva et al (2013) note that poetry slows time and heightens attention, 'thinks with feeling, awakens, and humanises us. Poems are not merely "flowers" but tools for creating' (p.71).

The following is a piece of my own poetry, written at a women's writing group session, which draws on my childhood experiences in Rotherham:

Child's play

Those endless summer days of wildness and freedom, that
we thought would never end, but they did all too soon for us
We played all day, and if we could we would have played all
night in those woods at the back of our houses, you and I
Rainy days in the sun, butterfly wings and candy clouds, a
new world to be discovered on our own doorstep, imagination
was to become our best friend
The long wild grass and fern beneath our feet in which we
played hide and seek, and the sweet smell of heather making
our noses itch
The kaleidoscope of flowers, bluebells, buttercups, wild
poppies and violets, evening primroses, dandelions and fox
gloves creating a perfumed garden for us to play in
Butterflies of multi-colours, floating over the splendid array
of flowers that lit up our eyes.

My poem contains elements of nostalgia. Boym (2001) states that:
'Nostalgia is yearning for a different time, the time of our childhood,
the slower rhythms of our dreams. In a broader sense, nostalgia is a
rebellion against the modern idea of time, the time of history and
progress' (p.8). I often think of the past, when the town of Rotherham
was a thriving industrial town. Over the years, we have seen a sad
decline and mass unemployment, and I do sometimes yearn for those
thriving days. Poetry helps to capture those feelings of loss and rapid
change, along with the disappearance of childhood.

Motapanyane (2013) argues that: 'poetry in the form of fieldwork
journal, is presented as a productive outlet for nostalgia, a method
of feminist self-reflexivity that can strengthen the researcher's crucial
intuition, clarity standpoint and interpretive approach and mediate
the condition of multiple belonging' (p12). My own writing in the
following poem reveals the power of nostalgia as a research method:

Dead town

The clear crystal blue sky of a Northern town, with no history
or heritage, the old is replaced by the new
Yesterday has gone and took with it all that was good
Closed steel factories, closed coal mines, closed hearts, empty
and hollow

No more massively tall industrial chimney's with smoke
blowing out of them, no power stations and cooling towers,
no more reminders of our past lives
No more community ties that bounded us together as one
The unbreakable chain of friendship, solidarity and common
purpose, lost

Looking back nostalgically at my childhood in Rotherham, I remember
the fun and excitement of being a child, of playing in the woods
at the back of my house until it became dark, or going to Clifton
Park in summer to listen to the colliery brass band playing every
Sunday afternoon. Eating fish and chips wrapped in old newspapers,
experiencing snow that went on for days and days and you thought
it would never stop. My poem 'Child's play' is a childhood reflection
and allows me to examine my identity. I was a daughter of a steel
worker and an outsider living in an industrial town, as my father was
an immigrant. I wanted desperately to be accepted and could not
understand why children at my school were not nice to me. Racism
and prejudice were not words in my vocabulary at that time; now
poetry has become a tool for challenging racism.

Feminism and poetry

Writing poetry enables women to put into words their anger and
frustration on gender inequality, the role of women in society. Poetry
creates a safe space for women and girls to write. Schutte (2011)
describes how 'women need a creative language of their own to write
their embodied position as women' (p.48). Poetry gives women an
opportunity to question patriarchy and women's role within society
at a given time, and reinforces the reality of women's lives. Poetry
also transcends time and connects different generations of women
together through their gendered experiences. An example of this,
which emerged during my work with writers in Rotherham, was the
point of school, the place where we are sent to be educated. School
can be a space for you to develop your mind and flourish, or it can be
a space where you are oppressed and denied. As Wendy Dasler Johnson
(2016) notes, 'Poetry might absorb a woman's pain' (p.42).

Here I reflect and share my experiences of school and education:

What did school teach me?

They tried to teach me to be a domestic goddess, a cross between dear old Mary Berry and the delightful Delia Smith, they failed badly I was never destined to be the next Nigella Lawson in the kitchen.

Needle work, it took me that long to make my baby sister's dress by the time I finished it, she had reached puberty, at least I did not become sewing factory fodder, up yours career's officer

Learning French, 'the language of love' was a disaster I was frog marched with little love to the art class after crucifying the French language once too often

How I dreaded Monday mornings Morris dancing, trust me to get a teacher who was obsessed with it and made us all look like twits

PE was a no goer; I was very creative with my excuses from malaria to typhoid, every week a new tropical disease

History was my passion; I was going to be the next Emily Pankhurst except I was too frightened of my father, even now I get the urge sometimes to handcuff myself to Rotherham town hall railings

Schools are powerful institutions. Paulo Freire (1985) argues that: 'embedded within all educational decisions are also assumptions about the nature of learning in general, the worthiness and capabilities of students from various social groups' (Ladson-Billing and Gillborn, 2004, p.181). At school, I had aspirations to be a teacher. However, my careers officer told me to get a job at a sewing factory near my home. His suggestion made me cry for weeks and knocked my confidence for years; he had crushed my aspirations. I am mortified to this day and I cannot look at a sewing machine without a reminder of that awful experience. This was a case where education broke me.

The arts are a methodology for challenging oppressions and power balance and give voice to women's discontentment and position in society. The Jamaican poet Jean 'Binta' Breeze challenged the language of White establishment: 'Let's not call it colonialism, that is an academic term. Let's call it what it is – international theft of resources and robbery of people's land. Colonialism doesn't say that' (Palmer, 1999, p.31). Black poets grapple with the language of the colonialists and give its true meaning from a Black vantage point.

Poetry as a research methodological research tool opens up conversation at a more personal, emic gaze, which means offering an insider interpretation of one's own cultural, linguistic or religious practices. I know the girls would not have expressed themselves through other methods in the way they have through poetry, as most of them were very shy and reserved. What may have otherwise been unsaid was articulated through written words.

One of the younger writing group participants (aged 13) wrote a humorous poem about school life. If I had engaged in more traditional social science techniques, like interviews, and just asked selected questions to the author of this poem, I would not have elicited such a descriptive view of school:

What is school like?
School is like a prison,
We can't leave.
School is like an island,
We are all trapped.
School is like a toilet,
It's full of germs.
School is like a baby,
It always needs your attention.
School is like a mother,
Who shouts all the time
School is full of bullies,
Who pick on you constantly
School is annoying however we need them to learn and be the people we would like to grow up to be.
Doctors, teachers, social workers.

Minority ethnic poets' voices

When the girls and women would meet for the writing groups, we often turned to minority ethnic women's poetry for inspiration, as we could relate to the cultural framework of the poets, the traditions, norms, beliefs and value systems.

Indian-born British poet Usha Kisore argues that poets influence the worldview, saying: 'the pen is mightier than the sword view' (Chaudhuri, 2014, p.5). She says: 'the art of writing is reactionary, in an oppressive environment, writing is resistance and subversion' (p.5). She further comments that her poetry is the poetry of an ethnic minority woman in the UK, personal and postcolonial, reflecting her life and experience, multiculturalism, women's rights and her stance on racism. Her writing exemplifies how arts methodology 'illuminates aspects of human conditions' (Leavy, 2015, p.4).

Debjani Chatterjee represents the diverse cultures and religions of South Asia through her poetry. She writes about the Hindu Gods, Islam, festivals, food, identity and language as well as challenging patriarchy and women's low status through her poems (Chatterjee, 1989). In her study, Kola Eke (2013) found that patriarchy was deeply entrenched in African women's poetry: 'their poems are tied together by sexist predicament, women suffering under the patriarchy burden of male superiority and dominance' (p.17).

Women have always challenged the unfair treatment of their gender through powerful words, and our daughters have to keep challenging when we are long gone. Poetry binds our past, present and future experiences in expressive and imaginative ways. Poetry can be a catalyst in creating a vision for a more hopeful future, as the girls' writing group articulated in their poems. For example, a 10-year-old participant wrote about her imagined future world:

The new world
The sun shines bright
The world begins again
Dancing and playing in the air.
Having too much fun, days go fast
Time passes away
In the new world I can bring time back and start again
I stay forever 10
Silver stars twinkling hello
The golden moon reaches out to shake my hand,
The breeze calls my name and says make a wish
I wish I can fly on clouds and never come down

Participatory arts practices such as poetry can provide a real body of knowledge to research. Furman (2006) suggested that: 'Poetry in particular has become a valuable tool for qualitative researchers' (p.560). Furman argues that: 'successful expressive poems are based on empirical data that are sensory and evocative in nature. Imagistic language allows the reader to enter a world and develop his or her own personal relationship with it; the images are transformed into knowledge' (p.561). Poetry weaves life trajectories like a spider's web; it maps in poetic language the long journey we have travelled to get to the present.

Poetry captures the immediacy of that moment before it is gone forever. One of the girls in the writing group (a 13-year-old participant) wrote about the rain. I remember the group met on a Saturday, it started to rain very heavily and she immediately started writing this verse:

The rainy weather
I love the rainy weather
I love rainy days because we all rush in for cover
Everyone is sitting in our home, chatting away
When it's rainy, we like to watch a movie and drink hot chocolate
The rain bring our family together
So let it rain more

Simecek (2015) argues that 'language articulates our feelings, makes them clearer and more defined, poetry enriches our emotional lives by allowing us to explore how our emotions arise from the particular perspective' (p.513). Poems capture everyday human interactions and give them a different meaning, enabling people to articulate human warmth and empathy. Poems can challenge discrimination against a particular social group, stigma of mental health for example. Certain themes emerged from the writing sessions, such as Islam and racism, and the poetry gave an insight into particular experiences.

The following is a poem I wrote and shared for the first time at the women's writing session during a very dismal October:

Winter blues
Voices in your head scream 'come out and play with your demons.'
While the hysterical clowns smirk at your misfortune and cry tears of sadness.
Madness ties you down to a lonely old existence without family and friends,
yet, you find solace in the world you have created where no one can reach you,
unless you open the door
You look up at the grey sky and think another long grey day ahead,
grey is becoming your best colour now that your rainbow disappeared

in to those grey clouds that thunder with rain in your head
You feel salty tears on your face and wonder how you got here,
your world although empty is still better than their superficial one,
    at least you don't have to justify your actions and conform to their norms.

Children and young people occupy a unique and complex world. Engaging them in poetry methodology enables a researcher to gain an understanding of their thoughts, feelings, moral judgements and values, and conscious and unconscious thoughts, which other methodologies may not capture. The youngest participant of the girls' writing group, 10 years old at the time, writes about a snail in her garden and her dilemma as to whether to let it live. I have the same dilemma with spiders in the bath: to drown or not to drown.

Snail
Slimy snail gliding across my window ledge
Leaving slime wherever it goes
Munching leaves on my plants.
And leaving the leaves with holes
What shall I do?
Should I kill it?
Should I mash it?
Should I kick it?
No because it is god's creature
I should leave it to enjoy life like me.

Imagining a better future

Poetry is not just for looking back nostalgically; it also allows us to present an imagined future of hope. It opens up possibilities for our mind to wonder to a different place and time.

Zalipour (2011) argues that: 'one feature that repeatedly emerges is the notion of imagination and the term "poetic imagination" to depict the emotional, imaginative, intellectual and the expressive language used to reflect the writer's consciousness' (p.481). The poetic imagination enables the visualisation of a future in front of us. One of the young participants of my writing group writes about an imagined future, a better world of 'flying in the air, jumping from cloud to cloud':

Dreaming a dream
Dreaming in my bed on a lazy day,
I see a picture in my mind of the world 100 years from now.
No one suffering, no poor, wealth is shared.
No illness and no disease
Peace with no wars and no fighting
Everyone is happy and helping each other through bad times
Fireworks lighting up a new morning
The sun shines and families gather together and celebrate
Sky scrapers of steel in the air
Children playing, flying in the air, jumping from cloud to cloud
How happy we will all feel inside
We shall live in peace
Forget the past and bring on the future.

Poetry is a methodological approach that can offer different modes of understanding that might not result from traditional methods of inquiry. It also places the researcher at the centre of the study. Poetry allows participants time to reflect on their inner human emotional experiences and to articulate those in their own particular way. Monica Pendergast argues:

> Poetic methods are qualitative and call for self-conscious participation. Instead of being inverted like a telescope for a distancing effect, poetics turns it back around for magnified encounters with life as lived, up close and personal, and sets it in a mode where everything reported is proprietary, overtly as the authors write about their presence in the research. (Prendergast et al, 2009, p.11)

For Rotherham's ethnic minority women, poetry has opened up a floodgate for women's writing and a new way of channelling feelings and lived experiences.

TWENTY

The Tassibee 'Skin and Spirit' project

Cassie Limb

The Tassibee 'Skin and Spirit' project

From meeting with Tassibee's Chief Executive Khalida Luqman (see Chapter Nine) Cassie Limb, artist, devised an arts programme in response to some of the concerns raised in the Jay Report (2014). The objectives were to work with a group of girls, aged between 7 and 19, with a focus on building their identity and confidence. The aim was to explore anti-bullying strategies through a range of group and individual art and creative activities for a three-month period.

'Skin and Spirit' was the title of our project. It was able to meet its aims through the exploration of the perception of what our cover of skin is holding 'within'. By creatively exploring what is valued and 'precious' and what is 'perceived', and through facilitating safe and open spaces to explore the girls' experiences, both negative and lovely. We focused on positive impressions of other people's behaviour, people that they had as their role models; kind and good-natured relatives were talked about, with important traits highlighted and made into a wire sculpture, and we explored and made connections to a variety of their mystical and cultural roots. Deep connections were made as Cassie led with a creative research approach, as opposed to rigid and structured course content. The incorporation of Tibetan singing bowls created the important conceptual link between understanding frequencies, thoughts, intentions and prayers by visually showing cymatic, or wave-like, patterns on water. This chapter has captured some of the dialogues and artworks from the sessions, with explanations of the activities. It finishes with a poem by Cassie in response to the project.

Precious boxes

The first creative session engaged the group straightaway, with the decorating of small boxes with glitter and fluorescent sand. The sparkly materials were placed inside the boxes, and dark decorated papers were used to cover the exteriors. At the end of the session, Cassie turned on an ultraviolet light, and the room was filled with the girls' exclamations of how each others' boxes were so beautiful.

These small 'precious boxes' explored their 'inner beauty', which could easily be tarnished, dulled or spoiled by others, if the individual or those around it cannot see how to value and protect it. The girls went on to express their feelings that it is only the individual who can experience this inner beauty to its fullest. Others may judge and stereotype; however, friends and family may get to see us sparkle and glow, if we feel safe and learn to shine.

Figure 20.1: 'Precious boxes' (outside)

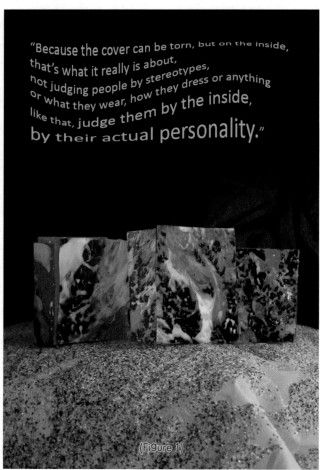

The following quotes capture some of the girls' interpretations of the activity:

> Like one of the famous sayings 'don't judge a book by its cover' because the cover can be torn, but on the inside, that's what it really is about, not judging people by stereotypes, or what they wear, how they dress or anything like that, judge them by the inside, by their actual personality.

> Until someone gets to know us they won't see the inner beauty that we see in ourselves.

> On the inside, no one can see that but you, you are special, everyone's beautiful on the inside, and you're the only one person can see it, and that's you.

Figure 20.2: 'Precious boxes' (inside)

'Time machines'

As the girls grew more comfortable with each other, their conversation flowed and turned to discussing their current personal situations. They shared their fears and worries about exams and results, marriage arrangements, expectations and life decisions that would impact on their futures. We turned these fears and unknowns into research questions:

- What does the future feel like?
- How different will I feel in the future?

To explore these research questions, the decision was made to make a 'time machine', which would allow the girls to visit their 'futures', to see what it would feel like once these decisions had been made and passed in time. In this way, the girls were inspired to engage creatively in using artistic approaches, while conducting research.

The 'time machine' was to be an interactive experience in the form of a large 'precious box', expanding on our earlier activity. It was to be big enough for one person to sit inside, decorated with glowing glitter on the inside, just like the small boxes, with fabric, bangles and wire words they had made previously on the outside. Using their imaginations, the girls agreed that when inside the box, the spirit would be instantaneously transported into the future; however, those on the outside could still communicate from their current place in time.

This inspired the group to develop further research questions they wanted to consider:

- Is the future written completely? Is it set in stone?
- Has it not happened?
- Does it make its way towards us or do we make our way towards it?
- Is the future changeable? Is it tangible? Is it transparent?
- How is, or will, the future be experienced? Or is it still building itself around us?

Conversations and interviews conducted from 'the future' arose from the group members asking questions from outside the box. The girls were surprised about how they felt like 'themselves' in the 'future'. The following are some of the reflections from the girls' experience of being in the 'future':

So also this concept of the future it doesn't exist, yep it doesn't because we don't know what is round the corner, we don't see it. We don't know what is going to happen so rather than just thinking about the future, just live the moment you're in, so you're worrying about the future you will spoil the moment we are living in, we just, we don't enjoy things we distract ourselves from like, we need to think about the things that make us happy. We just think oh what's going to happen in the future, we don't even know what the future holds for us, for God's sake just leave the future, and leave the past alone, just live the moment, just leave it, just live it!

I believe that we should live in the moment and we shouldn't think too much about the future, because thinking wouldn't take you anywhere.

I believe that most of the problems we think about we don't even encounter them. We just think about the future, this is going to happen, that is going to happen, you get to there, you probably won't even feel, face those problems, so we should make the most of the situation you are in, that is the only key to happiness, I believe.

The group's conclusion, having experienced the 'future', was that we can only exist in the 'now'. The girls pondered how else the future would arrive other than from our present location and our personal perception of 'now'.

We continued decorating the outside of the box and, during this process, the box became more representative of the physical 'body'. This notion allowed the girls to explore the separation between their 'inner' experiences and their 'outer' experiences. During the sessions, through their associations with the materials that were being used, it became apparent that this 'time machine' was becoming symbolic of a 'bride', through the making of bangles, and by affixing decorative fabrics and glitters. It was sensed and discussed that the fabrics and items used evoked much significance for the girls, expressing deeper, culturally rich meanings and emotive references. Here are the girls' interpretations:

The red fabric represents passion, blood and death.

It is also traditionally the colour worn in Asian weddings.

The pink inside represents the eternal inner child, pink being associated with baby girls, youth and childhood.

For those young women in the Tassibee project who were already married, these observations led them to sharing memories of their wedding day with the younger girls, while the unmarried girls imagined what it would be like for them. Girls in the group expressed sentiments regarding such futures in the following terms: 'mixed emotions', 'completely different life', 'new beginnings', 'leaving your family to go and live with a completely new family'.

The discussion of marriage led to a question being posed: 'Can you imagine growing up and having your own family?' This was beautifully answered by a younger girl; with a spread of her arm, encompassing her siblings, she simply stated: 'But I already have a family'. As we grow older we are more able to perceive ourselves in different situations, but this response highlighted the here and now for this young woman, which was very powerful and beautifully put.

Other thoughts expressed by the girls from inside the 'bride' version of the 'time machine' were:

It feels like you're in space.

People are very caught up in thinking that this (skin/body) is them, they don't realise that [it] is just our inside that counts, this is just the house, and the real thing is inside.

Thinking doesn't take you anywhere, just enjoy the moment you are in.

People stereotype and expect us to behave according to the box they put us in ... you are never going [to] please everyone.

Heptahedron 'planets'

Moving on from the 'precious box' activity, the girls turned to creating their own heptahedron artworks. The activity involved the girls, in pairs, decorating their heptahedrons with collage fragments from atlases, maps (making their own 'new lands') and with fluorescent glitter. They imagined their artworks to be new planetary bodies, inhabited

Figure 20.3: Heptahedron artworks

"I think that nirvana and utopia's do actually exist, but it's all the darkness in the world that's covering it up."

(Figure 3)

by individuals, whereby every grain of glitter represented a person, each shining with potential and beauty.

These creative activities led to conversations and appreciations for a community of beings, co-existing on planets created by the girls.

> I think that nirvana and utopias do actually exist, but it's all the darkness in the world that's covering it up, ... we just need to break away all that homophobic, racist stuff, break away that, and get to nirvana [and] utopia that everyone wishes, that everyone wants.

The room was darkened and ultraviolet lights were turned on to view the artworks all together. A solar system of planets glowed into existence, with the group in awe of their creations. The air was thick with excitement and appreciation for what the girls had made together. These moments were palpable – a buzz and connection was strengthening among the group too.

The research had evolved from exploring the individual to exploring the collective ties of the group through their group artwork, expanding their imaginations beyond Rotherham, yet grounding a new reality in shared imaginations. Through their collaborations in making these beautiful heptahedron artworks, they were mapping out new environments and connecting to concepts beyond where they lived. By expanding their thoughts beyond the physical bricks and mortar of the Tassibee centre, and then refocusing on their individual imaginations, they utilised materials, including the glowing ultraviolet lighting, to construct realities that were newly imagined environments.

In these moments, their hearts were activated, radiating feelings of excitement and connection at being expanded from their normally perceived reality. The girls expressed that they had the potential to generate beneficial effects for themselves and the wider community. By understanding and combining new concepts that grew from these feelings, the girls had begun to perceive the connection between their thoughts and their environment.

Tibetan singing bowl

To deepen this exploration, Cassie brought in her Tibetan singing bowl. Singing bowls are used as healing and meditation tools, originating from ancient India and Tibetan monasteries, and are now starting to be used more widely in the western world.

By adding water to the bowl, the girls experienced 'seeing' the sound vibrations, by pressing the rosewood baton on the outside edge and circling the bowl to create the sound. The girls could see that the water in the singing bowl creates patterns on the surface of the water, even when the audible ring had gone silent, and they could still feel the vibrations emanating when they touched the bowl when it was played.

This led to the group comprehending that silent frequencies can still be felt. This was a pivotal moment for the girls, as it led on to the idea that good intentions, including their prayers, were also silent frequencies, created by them, within their own bodies, which are 80 percent water. These were important moments, which connected the girls together in a collective experience, in contrast to their previous individual explorations of self. Through the concept of frequencies, the girls found a precious 'being' deep within their layer of skin, and explored the possibility that one's self could radiate beyond and emanate these positive vibrations out into their community environments. The dots they were connecting between themselves were forming foundations for continuing to build a community together, outside of our group arts project; in this community they could continue to choose to value and grow their cultural roots and practices.

> The Tibetan singing bowl personally to me, represents how two individuals together, who share our thoughts, opinions, our feelings, we can get this beautiful sound, this beautiful movement in the world.

The 'Skin and spirit' project delivered activities that were creative and playful, to engage the girls' imaginations. The girls were responsive. The project gave them the opportunity to re-imagine their community and find validation for their faith and cultural practices. It strengthened their desire to continue. This in turn created a confidence that was sown by themselves not by external or mainstream validation.

The project created opportunities for new discoveries as well as a safe space for the girls to express their frustrations, born out of the negative interactions they had experienced. They explored their own cultural perceptions openly, and looked at stereotyping and positive behaviour. There was joy expressed at making new connections, through creatively examining the essence of 'spirit,' through the making of 'precious boxes', decorating heptahedron platonic shapes and their very own 'time machine'. Taking part in these simple activities expanded the girls' connections and let in new realities of re-imagined selves, not previously perceived. They seemed more self-assured, genuinely confident and took ownership of what they were experiencing and creating. To see this transformation in such a short space of time was beautiful and became the inspiration for the following poem, written by Cassie. The poem also comments on various elements of current society and how the girls could be seen to shine.

Figure 20.4: Poem by Cassie Limb

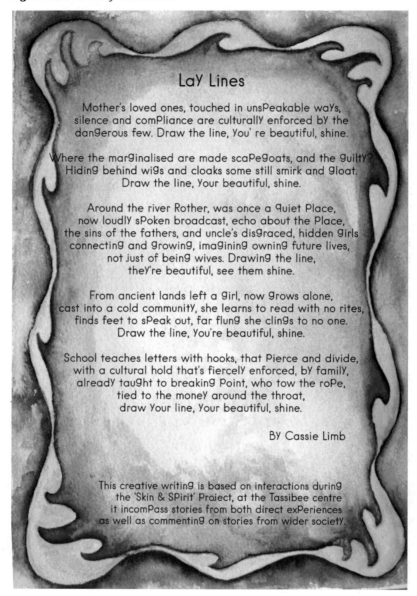

TWENTY-ONE

'The Rotherham project': young men represent themselves and their town

Nathan Gibson with Zanib Rasool and Kate Pahl

In the Rotherham project, photographer Nathan Gibson worked with a group of young men from a wide range of ethnic and cultural backgrounds (Pakistani, Yemeni, Afghan and White British). Participants were aged between 12 and 16, and were involved in youth projects at Rotherham United Community Sports Trust. The project aimed to use photography as a means of exploring identity and to investigate themes related to the ethics of representation, informed by the participants' first-hand experience of living in Rotherham.

The young men wanted to visit places new to them. They explored the town on foot and by minibus, visiting the town centre, the surrounding countryside and places of special interest, such as a local castle. During the photography sessions, the young men highlighted:

- the things they liked about Rotherham (football, interaction between communities, the importance of particular clothing within certain religious contexts, a love of nature and the rural environment);
- challenges they found concerning (an awareness of racism and violence within the town);
- their hopes for the future.

An awareness of tensions within the town and an enthusiastic appreciation of multicultural cohesion were repeatedly expressed by participants, and the diverse backgrounds of the young men were reflected in discussions during the sessions. The project allowed a space for those taking part to reflect on their perceived place within Rotherham, and highlighted that while there are elements of the town that they found problematic, there was also, in friendship and diversity, much to celebrate.

In reflective sessions following the photography trips, the group put photos on the wall and talked about their images, highlighting that the young men viewed their identity within the town as multifaceted, along many parallel and intersecting lines related to ethnic and religious identity, age, gender, community history, roots and geographical location. They displayed an extensive and detailed knowledge of different cultures within the town, and were able to openly discuss the differences and similarities they shared with one another. A youth centre provided the space for these discussions to happen outside the context of school, and the photographs produced acted as a visual catalyst for interactions that may not have happened otherwise. As young people in a multicultural environment, an element of fluidity was expressed with relation to group and individual identities, and intercultural diversity was generally accepted and celebrated as simply being part of their generation's experience of the world (see Figure 21.1: The boys).

Figure 21.1: The boys

When there is integration, there is mutual respect and tolerance. One young man took a lovely photograph of two boys with their arms around each other on a bus to school (see Figure 21.2: Friendship).

For this group of boys, diversity is the norm. School and friends are an important part of their everyday life and they took selfies of themselves and with their friends.

The issue of identity was particularly evident during a discussion in one of the early sessions. When viewing historical images of diverse groups, the boys discussed in a humorous way what they described as people 'dressing Asian'. Elaborating further, the boys described

Figure 21.2: Friendship

this clothing as what 'my Dad wears' and something they would only wear to Mosque or during family or cultural celebrations. Two boys in particular 'dressed Asian' on a regular basis, leading to a discussion around why people dress in certain ways at certain times, and how people's behaviour changes to suit the demands of the role the individual is playing. One boy who attended mosque each day felt that his faith was a cornerstone of his identity, seen clearly when, after each session, the boy was dropped off first so he could go to mosque. One week he asked if the group could accompany him to meet the Imam, displaying a pride in his faith that had not previously been seen in sessions. The ease with which he could adapt from a boisterous and enthusiastic sports fan to a quieter, thoughtful young man dedicated to his religious beliefs was notable, almost as if when he changed from his Manchester United football top into his Kurta, a new aspect of his identity emerged.

On a trip to Sheffield United and Sheffield Wednesday football clubs, participants photographed statues of famous footballers (see Figure 21.3: Sport). They visited KFC (a fast-food outlet) and discussed where they could get cheap food, displaying a considered understanding of finances and household budgets – a skill that has been developed outside the school environment.

Figure 21.3: Sport

The boys took many photographs of the natural world. One abstract image of a horse demonstrated an aesthetic awareness of beauty and the potential of photography to produce new and engaging views of the world (see Figure 21.4: Horse).

Figure 21.4: Horse

Figure 21.5: Spire

It was initially anticipated that participants would want to reflect in their photography their local community and feelings related to the many issues visible in the media. Instead, images produced provided an insight into individual and collective identity, how faith manifests itself in communities, and how friendships can cut across cultural divides (see Figure 21.5: Spire).

Young people's voices are often muted within mainstream culture. The project revealed everyday lived experiences through artistic methods in a way that represented anew the complexities of growing up in a culturally diverse space, while celebrating the strengths of community.

Part Four
Communities going forward

TWENTY-TWO

Re-imagining contested communities: implications for policy research

Robert Rutherfoord and Maria O'Beirne

We write this contribution as social researchers in the Department for Communities and Local Government (DCLG), the part of government responsible for housing, planning, local government, integration and communities policy for England. It is our role, as analysts, to bring evidence into the policy-making process.

This whole book has a wealth of insights and perspectives, which can contribute to a better understanding of communities and policy challenges at a local level. The content demonstrates the value of close and collaborative engagement with communities in a particular place to elicit, consider, negotiate and authentically represent the life worlds of people, using their own words and perspectives.

The mission of collaborative ethnography is to bring the academic research endeavour closer to communities, and to generate knowledge *together*, which is more authentic, representative and negotiated with communities. The questions of 'Whose knowledge?' and 'Who speaks for whom?' is an issue that should be asked of all research – and indeed all knowledge claims. In this book, we can see an emerging parity in the status of the different voices and knowledge presented.

We suggest that this example of collaborative ethnography could have even more impact if it were generated in collaboration with policy contributors, and it is notable that the local authority has worked in partnership with the 'Imagine' project in Rotherham. This points to other opportunities to bring together communities, local policy makers and academics in generating knowledge for future policy making.

Academic researchers play the key role in this collaborative enquiry process. They are strengthened by virtue of their institutional independence, methodological resources, and their theoretical frameworks and research tools. These can therefore provide partners with the means to sort and organise their personal experiences and accounts. The collective impact of such engagement is that people from different backgrounds may begin to find a common platform, take steps to challenge common understandings and misunderstandings, and even build a more shared future. This can contribute to the goals of supporting more integrated communities and of reducing community tensions – goals supported by many residents and by politicians of most political orientations.

How policy might fit into this more collaborative research endeavour is not clear-cut. There is no one single policy maker or institution to involve who has a 'command and control' impact on local communities; rather, a network of interlocking organisations within a policy-making system. This network shifts and has changed form over the decades. Recent shifts have sought to reduce control from the centre ('Whitehall'), and have placed more emphasis on devolution – local autonomy and community empowerment (Wills, 2016). This has also been accompanied by a move towards 'Open Policy Making' (Cabinet Office, 2016), which seeks to stimulate a wider conversation about policy involving stakeholders, experts and users (Kimbell and MacDonald, 2015). The implications of this are that while policy responsibility has become more diffuse, it has become, in principle, more open. It is at the local level where the main interventions and political representation that impacts on communities are to be found. Even when policy making is more centrally initiated, it still requires local interpretation and implementation.

There is also a vision for a more collaborative approach to policy–citizen interaction. This is often described as 'co-production', which values local knowledge and a more equal partnership between 'policy makers' and those who are the objects of policy. This involves rebalancing and challenging the implied hierarchy between 'expert' and 'lay' knowledge, and engendering ways of treating communities, and community knowledge, as an asset (see Durose and Richardson, 2016, pp.42-7). This way of thinking can be applied to all forms of public policy – and to the delivery of public services at neighbourhood level in particular.

Therefore, the policy community can be a collaborator in the generation of local knowledge, and local voices a collaborator in the generation of policy. This type of connectivity is well supported by evidence and through relationships nurtured by collaborative research.

If community-based collaborative research is to make its full impact, then it would need to develop beyond a small number of case study areas and be strategically planned, resourced and structured. This inevitably brings us back to questions about how – and what type of – academic research is prioritised, and how research careers are incentivised to include more collaborative, community-based knowledge production. Gathering more information, or evaluation of, how collaborative research impacts on communities, community cohesion and wellbeing might be one way to demonstrate the value of this kind of activity.

There are hundreds of towns, cities and regions in the country that could potentially benefit from this kind of research model – though how to structure that collaboration in such a way that it is effectively resourced and feeds into policy making is a real challenge. In previous decades (in the 1960s and 1970s in particular), community studies were more commonplace (Allan and Phillipson, 2008), but they have fallen out of favour as the demand for more indirect empirical and statistical evidence has achieved primacy in policy-making circles.

We think that there is scope for a mixture of approaches, including place-based collaborative inquiry, to understand the complexity of the dynamics of contemporary communities and to inform and enrich policy making. This is particularly important where the policies focus on social relationships, social interaction, and social and civic action. This book therefore provides a valuable resource, not only in terms of its content, but also in its insights into methods of evidence generation and collaborative working between universities, communities and policy makers.

TWENTY-THREE

What this book can teach us

*Elizabeth Campbell, Kate Pahl, Elizabeth Pente
and Zanib Rasool*

Our central goal in writing this book has been to demonstrate that communities produce their own forms of knowledge, and that those forms are valid – and valuable – ways of knowing. We set out to articulate the value of this kind of research for community knowledge production that is emergent, situated and future oriented.

We asked readers to keep these questions in mind as they read:

- Whose voices count in collaborations and why?
- What kinds of voices do artistic modes of enquiry let in?
- How do we incorporate diverse voices in research?
- What are the limitations of linguistically oriented research methods?
- What do you do when you don't agree?
- How does history contribute to an understanding of communities in the everyday?
- How do places emerge in our minds?
- What kinds of experiences shape the way we understand place?
- Can places change and how do they change?
- How can universities make things better in some way?

In this final reflection, we offer our readers a sense of the legacy of this book and identify its key features, in order to provide a summary of what we have learned from doing the book. We can identify four key themes:

- thinking across difference;
- the arts as a mode of inquiry and as an agent of change;
- rethinking knowledge production practices;
- hope and the importance of transformational change.

Here we offer our thoughts on these themes.

Thinking across difference

A multiplicity of voices contributes to a more complex and nuanced lens that is much needed. That voice is not single and unitary and this is important to recognise. In their work highlighting the diversity of writing in cities such as Bradford and London, Mcloughlin (2014) observe that writing about British Asian cities is 'complex, often ambivalent, [and] potentially counter-hegemonic'. Part of this is a lack of consideration in some archival work of particular histories, and the issue of 'important gaps, silences and discrepancies in the archive. This results in a more complex and subtle, if still inevitably incomplete, analysis of British Asian cities and their representation (McLoughlin, 2014, p.2). Our research resists certainty – while engaging strongly with lived realities, we acknowledge difference and dissensus within our work.

The arts as a mode of inquiry and as an agent of change

The arts open up alternative spaces for voices to be surfaced. In this book, the voices of young people come to the fore, as well as those of artists. The original 'Case for Support' for the 'Imagine' project talked about the possibilities in the arts:

> We hold faith with the power of the arts to promote social resilience and renewal – not as an abstract blueprint but as a small-scale, place-based materialisation out of which a productively critical and collaborative response to the present can be pursued. In this proposal, the concept of 'imagined future' declares a space where creativity is both a site of resistance to, and escape from, pessimistic social scripts and is always tied to a politics and practice of present hope. (Case for Support, 'Imagine', 2011)

Many of the chapters use poetry and the arts to surface hidden knowledge and to confront uncomfortable truths. The concept, described above, of creativity as a way to counter pessimism has certainly been important in this book. Many of the chapters provide a very different counter-narrative to dominant discourses about Rotherham, producing complex accounts of hopeful literacies of resistance and celebration. For example, when exploring narratives of hope with Roma heritage young people, it was possible to create new scripts for what 'could be'. These can empower young people as they move forward in their lives. The arts can enable these voices to come to the fore.

Untold stories can also be told through art, as artist Shahin Shah eloquently articulates. This book explores hidden histories in a multiplicity of ways and within many voices and modes of description. Artistic methods surface tacit and embodied ways of knowing, they can unsettle, confuse but also alert us to new scripts and ways of knowing. Our work celebrates these complex narratives of hope and encounters with the lived experience of the everyday. This then recreates knowledge production practices within visual and located modes of engagement. These move and transform themselves in the process of making.

Rethinking knowledge production practices

Co-production across this book takes many forms – it is enacted in exhibitions, books, discussions, projects, ideas and this book. It offers a way of expanding what 'counts' as knowledge, beyond that which is produced in universities. In exploring community histories of Rotherham, this book has highlighted some of the ways in which communities are working to address the absences of their histories in official archival records, through heritage projects, poetry, arts practice and creative artefacts, connecting oral traditions with objects, exploring private and public stories and in creative and reflective writing.

Through these examples, marginalised voices are brought to the fore, and demonstrate the valuable knowledge that emerges when engaging in co-production methodologies. The community histories presented in this volume therefore contribute to creating a different sense of history; one that challenges traditional power structures that construct history from a particular perspective. We hope that this work inspires others to consider the possibilities of co-production, and what can emerge from different types of histories, knowledge and forms of co-production.

The process of writing this book has made us re-look at the rich and diverse knowledge held by communities like Rotherham, and the importance of preserving heritage and cultural knowledge and literacy practices of the 'other' in a changing and somewhat turbulent world. Sometimes it is a lonely path as you fight your conscience to do justice to the communities you research. We will explain how certain theories are nested within the 'Imagine' project and within this book.

Many of the chapters in this book are concerned with the experiences of girls and women. They are gender specific, such as the sharing of herbal remedies, as women tend to be the ones trying to preserve their history, heritage and mother language. Mills (2004), in her study of language attitudes of bilingual mothers in the Midlands in the United Kingdom, found that some mothers felt a great sense of sadness at the loss of heritage language and wanted their children to retain their mother tongue and know their roots, and it was often left to the mother to promote the heritage language so the children know where their roots are. 'Women are responsible for nurturing a language within the families and are guardian of a culture' (Mills, 2008, p.165). Many of the chapters in this book are located within feminist theory, advocate for women's knowledge and offer a place in research to women's emotions. Our joint research gave their everyday lived knowledge and literacy practices recognition.

Our research in this book is also specific. Ann Oakley rightly argues that 'women and other minority groups, above all, need qualitative research because without this, it is difficult to distinguish between personal experience and collective oppression' (Oakley, 2005, p.189). Minority women share collective gender experience with other women, but they also face different obstacles such as racism, which the women and the girls we worked with on 'Imagine' write about eloquently.

As a Muslim woman, I (Zanib) feel that we are stigmatised by policy and media. The 'Imagine' project research gave us a voice to challenge and offered a different lens of understanding to our lives, so we become less invisible. Writing this book has given me the opportunity, as a minority ethnic woman, to undertake research within my own community. bell hooks (1984), in her writing on feminist theory and feminist movement, says 'it is essential that Black women recognise the special vantage point our marginality gives us and make use of this perspective to criticise the dominant racist, classist, sexist hegemony and create a counter hegemony' (p.2). British/Pakistani Muslim women occupy a different vantage point, for example, what some might see as oppressive, like the wearing of the hijab. The girls participating in the 'Imagine' project challenged that, saying it was their 'choice' and that they felt protected when wearing the hijab. We can offer counter-narratives from our particular vantage point.

During the writing of this book, there was a rise in Islamophobia, racism and women feeling unsafe. We created 'in between spaces', safe spaces where they could share their cultural knowledge and social literacy practices. Bhabha (1994) argues that 'in between spaces' provide a terrain for elaborating strategies of selfhood (p.2). The Muslim women and girls through their writing as described in this book are renegotiating their place in society, post-Brexit, post-Trump. These 'in between' or third spaces can create learning environments that leave behind the colonial history of oppression and offer a more equitable space for minority women to create their own knowledge. The women wrote poetry in their first language without being spoken down to like a child for not speaking and writing in English.

Our work in this book recognises diversity and difference. The late Brian Street argues for a more culturally sensitive approach to literacy, a refreshing perspective in a culture where we judge people illiterate too hastily:

> Researchers instead of privileging the particular literacy practices familiar to their own culture need to suspend judgement as to what constitutes literacy among the people they are working with until they are able to understand what it means to the people themselves, and which social contexts reading and writing derive their meaning from. People who may be labelled illiterate with the autonomous model of literacy may, from culturally sensitive viewpoint, be seen as making significant use of literacy practices for specific purposes and in specific contexts. (Street, 2005, p.14)

Third spaces are hybrid spaces and hubs for community 'funds of knowledge' and for transforming learning; we created these spaces in a community library, and in a school. Moje et al (2004), exploring multiple communities of practice and spaces linking to literate social, and cultural aspects of text, identity and sense of self, argue that: 'The notion of hybridity can apply to the integration of competing knowledge and discourses' (p.42). The women described in Chapter Thirteen shared their family herbal remedies, passed down through generations by word of mouth, and produced booklets with pictures to share with others, blending orality and text with images off the internet, advocating multimodel literacies. These unique practices were illuminated through our research and challenged the notion of 'illiterate', if one does not speak English. Informal learning spaces offer flexibility and empower the learner, by recognising existing knowledge that minority ethnic women possess, and giving it value.

Our book is an expression of the experiences of communities who have struggled to come to terms with an intensification of racism. Race and racism have been always there in our society and for a while multiculturalism gave us a false sense of security, but racism is a poison that is spreading through America and Europe today. The girls and women in this book wrote about their racialised world and of their experiences of racism. As a Muslim woman undertaking this research and in writing this book, I (Zanib) have provided an insider lens to our collective experiences.

Minority ethnic women are good at preserving traditional knowledge, passed through generations, and are guardians of such knowledge. Many households in my community still try family herbal remedies for minor ailments. Yet, the Western physicians would have once scorned the knowledge of herbalism. However, the West has now taken that knowledge and has represented as its own. Tuhiwai-Smith (1999) has talked about how indigenous knowledge has been colonised by the West, who take ownership of what they have learned, for example from the Maori communities, and argues that knowledge about indigenous people is 'collected, classified and represented in various ways back to the West, and through the eyes of the West back to those who have colonised' (p.31). Research in Western Alaska by indigenous communities highlighted that there was still a 'lack of a voice for indigenous people who were are often left in the dark' (Yakoubian and Yakoubian, 2017, p.5). I strongly advocate that the knowledge within a community belongs to the community, and they should decide how it is disseminated and shared with the West.

Race is a key theme in our book. As Ladson-Billings and Tate once said, 'race continues to be a significant factor in determining inequalities in United States' (Ladson-Billings and Tate, 1995, p.48). Sadly it still does, as evidenced by the rise in Islamophobia and Muslim women being portrayed negatively and blamed for not integrating in society. Religion has become a determining factor for injustice in the US, in the UK and in Europe, and yet no one looks at the society that rejects and disempowers them.

The challenge for us as researchers is to develop an empowered model of scholarship. Mahuika, describing the experience of Maori researchers, focuses on indigenous ways of knowing, from the indigenous perspective of the world. Mahuika (2008) talks of the damage to Maori communities done by white researchers who have disempowered his people and have taken their knowledge and claimed it as their own, making themselves authorities on Maori culture. Mahuika says the Maori people started to fight back and wanted to safeguard their own knowledge and culture and have set up their own academic institutions. Mahuika talks of Kaupapa Maori Theory, a concept and practice of active resistance to the colonisation of Maori people and culture. This looks from a different epistemological tradition, which frames the way Maori people see the world, and asserts Maori cultural beliefs and way of knowing. He argues that Kaupapa Maori Theory provides a 'platform from which Maori are striving to articulate their own reality and experiences, and their own person truth' (p.4).

An empowered model of scholarship would recognise diversity, while acknowledging the power imbalances that cut across different perspectives. In this book, we have highlighted voices that sometimes do not get heard, in an attempt to redress this balance.

Hope and the importance of transformational change

This book teaches us hope, and that if we hold on and keep fighting, better days will come our way. Communities are coming together in solidarity, the good people uniting against the rhetoric of hate and challenging those who divide us. When people come together, good things will happen in those in between spaces, where we shall continue to keep diversity alive.

In 2011, we were in a different place, in what seemed a more stable world. Today, in my beloved town of Rotherham on 8 July 2017, I saw the very best of Rotherham coming together at our first 'MelAsia' event. It was 'a celebration of colour, culture and community', creating community cohesion through music, dance, food, sport, art and cultural activities.

People from all backgrounds are coming together, talking and reclaiming their town from the Far Right. I (Zanib) sat in Clifton Park with my brother's granddaughter and felt a great sense of pride in my town and for the people of Rotherham. It took me back to when I was her age, seven, sitting near the bandstand, listening to the colliery brass band. Today the music may have been more diverse, but that old familiar feeling of warmth and love surrounded me and my seven-year-old great-niece. That is the legacy we have to leave behind for our children, grandchildren and communities – so they can imagine a better world in their future.

Living within change and policy: whose voice is heard in that process?

Although this book is published, and to an extent finished, it represents an ongoing set of commitments and relationships. It is more than the edges of the page, more than a publication. The writing enacts a coming together of many voices. This book is an invitation to the reader to step into and out of the page, and to recognise that the multiple stories and perspectives that we encounter move through and beyond the page.

This book is not a museum of captured thoughts; it is a town full of people, getting on with things.

First, it features, in robust and full-throated ways, the voices of underrepresented and disenfranchised voices; yes, from a small to mid-sized town in South Yorkshire, but the featuring of these voices makes a general statement about the importance of listening to all voices in a democracy, or any form of society, for that matter. Second, this work illustrates how arts and humanities can be used as vehicles for learning, coming across difference, and social justice and change.

When we began this project in 2013, we did not anticipate the world this book would be born into. Back then, it was easier to believe that reasonable forces would prevail; that the anger, resentment and nativism/racism then rising would diminish or, at the very least, be contained. Our task, we thought, was simply to show how our work together offered ways to imagine stronger communities, and to create better futures.

But that tide is still building, rather than receding. We do not yet know if or when it will crash, nor the damage it will do when it does; our societies, it is beginning to seem, are in as much trouble as our ecosystems. The task now for all of us – writers and readers alike – is to somehow interrupt that tide, to defuse the crisis, to cultivate the desire for healing. Running throughout this project – indeed, through all of these many 'Imagine' projects – is the idea that communities and universities, working together, can make stronger societies. There is a greater urgency to this idea now than there has ever been for us; if we want to see the better societies we imagine, we must all, each in our own ways, begin the work of creating them.

For us, that means doing the very real and difficult work of working across our differences, without eschewing them. Working across difference begins with respect, and with a shared commitment or cooperatively imagined outcome, but it goes much further. It demands committed action, that we share the company of people who think, act and believe differently from us, because it is in those places that we are challenged to think differently. Those who participated in this project sought not to avoid, nor shut down, nor prioritise, nor naively celebrate difference. As best we could, we recognised and acknowledged our varied experiences, ideas, priorities and beliefs, creating respectful and productive spaces, where those differences could bump up against each other, producing a new, richer and much more complex kind of knowledge.

The core value of collaboration has animated this project throughout, and informed the methods of collaborative ethnography used within.

In *Doing ethnography today*, Campbell and Lassiter (2015) observe that this kind of research has 'the potential to transform ourselves, others, and even the communities in which we live and work ... and that it can thus be an act of peace (however modest or small) in a world wrought with misunderstanding, conflict, and violence' (p.9).

We collectively acknowledge that our book enacts the process. It is as much about the experience of working with different people as much as the knowledge that comes out of that experience. This book shows how one group of people have used the opportunity of research to deepen their experience of each other and their understandings of each other's differences. They have come away from the experience with an understanding of how each other works. We have shared experiences, and learned to listen in new ways to each other's truths. We are not the same, but collectively we can acknowledge and realise difference in a way that offers hope for a better future. We have to, in Emily Dickinson's words,[1] 'tell all the truth, but tell it slant':

> Tell all the truth but tell it slant —
> Success in Circuit lies
> Too bright for our infirm Delight
> The Truth's superb surprise
> As Lightning to the Children eased
> With explanation kind
> The Truth must dazzle gradually
> Or every man be blind
>
> (Emily Dickinson)

Note

[1] Reproduced with permission from: *The Poems of Emily Dickinson: Variorum Edition*, edited by Ralph W. Franklin, Cambridge, Mass.: The Belknap Press of Harvard University Press. Copyright © 1998 by the President and Fellows of Harvard College. Copyright © 1951, 1955 by the President and Fellows of Harvard College. Copyright © renewed 1979, 1983 by the President and Fellows of Harvard College. Copyright © 1914, 1918, 1919, 1924, 1929, 1930, 1932, 1935, 1937, 1942 by Martha Dickinson Bianchi. Copyright © 1952, 1957, 1958, 1963, 1965 by Mary L. Hampson.

References

Age Concern Rotherham (2007) *Rotherham Reminiscences: An oral history project recording the memories and experiences of clients during World War II.* www.ageuk.org.uk/rotherham/news--campaigns/rotherham-reminiscences/

Ahmed, S. (2004) *The Cultural Politics of Emotion*, London: Routledge.

Ajegbo, K. (2007) *Diversity and Citizenship: Curriculum review.* Department for Education and Skills.

Allan, G. and Phillipson, C. (2008) Community studies today: urban perspectives, *International Journal of Social Research Methodology*, 11, 2, 163-73.

Al-Muneera (2007) *Their Lives, Our History*, Rotherham: Al-Muneera.

Al-Muneera (2011) *Sheffield: City of steel. South Asian men's contribution to the steel industry in South Yorkshire.* Rotherham: Al-Muneera.

Alba, R. and Nee, V. (1997) Rethinking assimilation theory for a new era of immigration, *The International Migration Review*, 31, 4, 836-74.

Appiah, A. K. (2006) *Cosmopolitanism Ethics in a World of Strangers*, Penguin Books Ltd.

Archer, L. (2001) Muslim brothers, Black lads, traditional Asian: British Muslim young men's constructions of race, religion and masculinity, *Feminism & Psychology*, 11, 1, 79-107.

Asad, T. (1973) *Anthropology & the Colonial Encounter*, New York: Humanities Press.

Avineri, N., Johnson, E., Brice-Heath, S., McCarty, T., Ochs, E., Kremer-Sadlik, T., Blum, S., Zentella, A.C., Rosa, J., Flores, N., Samy Alim, H., Paris, D. (2015) Invited forum: bridging the "language gap", *Journal of Linguistic Anthropology*, 25, 1, 66-86.

Back, L. and Puwar, N. (eds) (2012) *Live Methods*, Oxford: Blackwell Publishing.

Baggini, J. (2007) *Welcome to Everytown: A journey into the English mind*, London: Granta Books.

Beebeejaun, Y., Durose, C., Rees, J., Richardson, J. and Richardson, L. (2014) Beyond text: exploring ethos and method in co-producing research with communities, *Community Development Journal*, 49, 1, 37-53.

Benenson, J. and Stagg, A. (2015) An asset based approach to volunteering: exploring benefit of low income volunteers, *Non Profit and Voluntary Sector Quarterly*, 45 (IS), 1315-495.

Bhabha, H.K. (1994) *The Location of Culture*, Abingdon, Oxon: Routledge.

Bhattacharya, H. (2008) 'New critical collaborative ethnography', in Nagy, S., Hesse-Biber, S. and Levy, P. (eds) *Handbook of Emergent Methods*, New York: Guilford Press, 303-22.

Bourn, D. (2008) Young people, identity and living in a global society, *Policy and Press - A Development Education Review*, 7, 48-61.

Boym, S. (2001) 'Nostalgia and its discontent', in Boym, S. (ed.) *The Future of Nostalgia*, New York: Basic Books.

Brah, A. (1996) *Cartographies of Diaspora: Contested identities*, London and New York: Routledge.

Brettell, C. (1993) *When They Read What We Write: The politics of ethnography*, Westport, CT: Bergin and Garvey.

Breunlin, R. and Regis, H. A. (2009) Can there be a critical collaborative ethnography? Creativity and activism in the Seventh Ward, New Orleans, *Collaborative Anthropologies*, 2, 115-46.

Bright, G. (2012) A practice of concrete Utopia? Informal youth support and the possibility of 'redemptive remembering' in a UK coal-mining area, *Power and Education*, 4, 3, 314-26.

Brown, P. and Ferguson, I. T. (1995) Making a big stink: women's relationship, and toxic waste activism, *Gender and Society*, 9, 2, 145-72.

Cabinet Office (2016) *Open Policy Making Toolkit*. https://www.gov.uk/guidance/open-policy-making-toolkit/getting-started-with-open-policy-making

Campbell, E. and Lassiter, L. E. (2010) From collaborative ethnography to collaborative pedagogy: reflections on the other side of Middletown Project and community-university research partnerships, *Anthropology & Education Quarterly*, 41, 4, 370-85.

Campbell, E. and Lassiter, L. E. (2015) *Doing Ethnography Today*, Oxford: Wiley-Blackwell.

Carby, H. V. (1996) 'White women listen! Black feminism and the boundaries of sisterhood', in Baker, A. H. Jr, Diawara, M. and Lindeborg, R. H. (eds) *Black British Cultural Studies: A reader*, 110-28.

Carter, P. (2004) *Material Knowledge*, Melbourne: University of Melbourne Press.

Casey, L. (2016) *The Casey Review: A review into opportunity and integration*, Department for Communities and Local Government, https://www.gov.uk/government/uploads/system/uploads/attachment_data/file/575973/The_Casey_Review_Report.pdf

Cavaye, J. (n.d.) *Understanding community development*, Covaye Community Development, 1-20.

Centre for Hidden Histories, The (2014) http://hiddenhistorieswwi.ac.uk/about/

Charles, N. and Crow, G. (2012) Community re-studies and social change, *Special Issue of Sociological Review*, 60, 3, 399-404.

Charlesworth, S. (2000) *A Phenomenology of Working-Class Experience*, Cambridge: Cambridge University Press.

Chatterjee, D. (1989) *I Was That Woman*, London: Hippopotamus Press.

Chaudhuri, S. (2014) I, the dark woman, in the trajectory of your consciousness: Indian born British poet Usha Kishore in conversation with Sutapa Chaudhuri, *Writers in Conversation*, 1, 2, 1-10.

Checkoway, B. (2013) Social justice approach to community development, *Journal of Community Practice*, 24, 4, 472-86.

Christensen, P. and O'Brien, M. (2003) 'Place, space and knowledge: Children in the village and the city', in Christensen, P. and O'Brien, M. (eds) *Children in the city: Home neighbourhood and community*, London/New York: RouledgeFalmer Taylor & Francis Group, 13-28.

Churchill, H. and Clarke, K. (2009) Investing in parenting education: a critical review of policy and provision in England, *Social Policy & Society*, 9, 1, 39-53.

Clark, A. (2013) 'The history wars', in Clark, A. and Ashton, P. (eds) *Australian History Now*. Sydney: NewSouth, 151-66.

Clarke, K. (2006) Childhood, parenting and early intervention: A critical examination of the Sure Start national programme, *Critical Social Policy*, 26, 4, 699-721.

Clifford, J. (1983) On ethnographic authority, *Representations*, 2, 118-46.

Cohen, S. (2011) *Folk Devils and Moral Panic* (4th edn), Routledge, Taylor & Francis Group.

Cole, I. and Robinson, D. (2003) *Somali Housing Experience in England*. Centre for Regional Economic and Social Research. www4. shu.ac.uk/research/cresr/sites/shu.ac.uk/files/somali-housing-experiences-england.pdf

Conteh, J. and Brock, A. (2010) "Safe spaces"? Sites of bilingualism for young learners in home, school and community, *International Journal of Bilingual Education and Bilingualism*, 14, 3, 347-60.

Craith, N. M. (2006) *Europe and the politics of language: Citizens, migrants and outsiders*, Basingstoke: Palgrave Macmillan.

Crow, G. and Hart, A. (2012) "Our work is about trying to create democratic learning spaces": An interview with Angie Hart, Community University Partnership Programme, University of Brighton, *Collaborative Anthropologies*, 5, 125-41.

Crow, G. and Mah, A. (2012) *Conceptualisations and Meanings of 'Community': The theory and operationalization of a contested concept*. AHRC Connected Communities. www.ahrc.ac.uk/documents/project-reports-and-reviews/connected-communities/conceptualisations-and-meanings-of-community-the-theory-and-operationalization-of-a-contested-concept/

Darnell, R. (2001) *Invisible Genealogies: A history of Americanist anthropology*, Lincoln: University of Nebraska Press.

Department for Communities and Local Government (DCLG) (2007) *What Works' in Community Cohesion: Research Study conducted for Communities and Local Government and the Commission on Integration and Cohesion*, London: DCLG .

Dick, M. (2011) 'Locality and diversity: minority ethnic communities in the writing of Birmingham's local history', in Dyer, C., Hopper, A., Lord, E. and Tringham, N. (eds) *New Directions in Local History Since Hoskins*, Hatfield: University of Hertfordshire Press.

Dick, M. and Dudrah, R. (2011) Ethnic minority histories in the Midlands, *Midland History*, 36, 2, 143-48.

Dixon, P. (n.d.) '50 reasons to be proud'. https://englishpatriot.co.uk/2014/05/17/50-reasons-to-be-proud/#more-2133

Durose, C. and Richardson, L. (2016) *Designing Public Policy for Co-production: Theory, practice and change*, Policy Press, Bristol.

Eke, K. (2013) Response to patriarchy in African women's poetry, *Matatu: Journal for African Culture & Society*, 14, 1, 1-18.

Emerald, E. and Carpenter, L. (2015) Vulnerability and emotions in research: risks, dilemmas and doubts, *Qualitative Inquiry*, 21, 8, 741-50.

Eva, A.L., Bemis C.A., Quist. M.F., and Hollands. B. (2013) The Power of the Poetic Lens: Why Teachers Need to Read Poems Together, *The Journal of the Assembly for Expanded Perspective of Learning*, 19, X, 62-78.

Fabian, J. (1983) *Time and the Other: How anthropology makes its object*, New York: Columbia University Press.

Facer, K. and Enright, B. (2016) *Creating Living Knowledge: The connected communities programme, community-university partnerships and the participatory turn in the production of knowledge*, Bristol: University of Bristol/AHRC Connected Communities Programme.

Fanon, F. (1961) *The Wretched of the Earth*, New York, NY: Grove Press.

Faubion, J. D. and Marcus, G. E. (2009) *Fieldwork is Not What It Used To Be: Learning anthrolopology's method in a time of transition*, Ithaca, NY: Cornell University Press.

Field, F. (2010) *The Foundation Years: Preventing poor children becoming poor adults*, London: Cabinet Office, HM Government, http://www.poverty.ac.uk/sites/default/files/attachments/The%20Foundation%20Years%20preventing%20poor%20children%20becoming%20adults.pdf.

Field, L. W. (2008) *Abalone Tales: Collaborative explorations of sovereignty and identity in native California*, Durham: Duke University Press.

Finnegan, R. (2015) *Where is Language? An anthropologist's questions on language, literature and performance*, London: Bloomsbury Academic.

Flinders, D. (2009a) 'I remember when Rotherham was good: Part 1.' https://www.youtube.com/watch?v=9MG2n1w_hP0

Flinders, D. (2009b) 'Old Rotherham: Part 2. When England had an identity.' https://www.youtube.com/watch?v=fZT-NtW6uUk

Freire, P. (1985) The Politics of Education: Culture, Power and Liberation, in Ladson–Billings, G. and Gillborn, D. (eds) (2014) *The RouledgeFalmer Reader In Multicultural Education*, London: RoutledgeFalmer.

Fryer, P. (2010) *Staying Power: The history of Black people in Britain* (2nd edn), London: Pluto.

Furman, R. (2006) Poetic forms and structures in qualitative health research. *Qualitative Health Research*, 16, 4, 560-66.

Gale, R. (2014) 'Between the city lines: towards a spatial historiography of British Asian Birmingham', in Mcloughlin, S., Gould, W., Kabir, A.J. and Tomalin, E. (eds) *Writing the City in British Asian Diasporas*, London: Routledge, 114-34.

Getz, D. (2010) The nature and scope of festival studies, *International Journal of Event Management Research*, 5, 1, 1-47.

Gilchrist, A. (2009) *The Well Connected Community: A networking approach to community development* (2nd edn), Bristol: Policy Press, University of Bristol.

Gillies, V. (2007) *Marginalised Mothers. Exploring working-class experiences of parenting*, Oxon: Routledge.

Gilroy, P. (1987) *'There Ain't No Black in The Union Jack': The cultural politics of race and nation*, London: Unwin Hyman Press.

Godwin J, Jasper, J.M. and Polletta, F. (eds) (2001) *Passionate politics: Emotions and social movements*, Chicago: University of Chicago Press.

Gonzalez, N., Moll, L. C., Floyd-Tenery, M., Rivera, A., Rendon, P., Gonzalez, R. and Amanti, C. (1999) *Teacher Research on Funds of Knowledge: Learning from households*, Center for Research on Education, Diversity and Excellence, UC Berkeley.

Gould, W. and Qureshi, I. (2014) 'South Asian histories in Britain: Nation, locality and marginality', in McLoughlin, S., Gould, W., Kabir, A. J., Tomalin E. (eds) *Writing the City in British Asian Diasporas*, London: Routledge, 137-57.

Grainger, K. (2013) "The daily grunt": middle-class bias and vested interests in the 'Getting in Early' and 'Why Can't They Read?' reports, *Language and Education*, 27, 2, 99-109.

Gray, B. (2011) Empathy, emotion and feminist solidarities, *Critical Studies*, 34, 1, 207-232.

Hackett, A. (2017) Parents as researchers: Collaborative ethnography with parents, *Qualitative Research*, 17, 5, 481-497.

Hanley, L. (2007, 2012) *Estates: An intimate history* (2nd edn), London: Granta Books.

Hardyment, C. (2007) *Dream Babies. Childcare advice from John Locke to Gina Ford*, London: Frances Lincoln Ltd.

Hart, B. and Risley, T. R. (2003) The early catastrophe: The 30 million word gap by age 3, *American Educator*, 27, 1, 4-9.

Haviland, M. (2017) *Side by Side?: Community art and the challenge of co-creativity*, New York, NY: Routledge.

Heath, S. B. (1983) *Ways with Words: Language, life, and work in communities and classrooms*, Cambridge University Press.

Helm, T. (2016) Brexit Britain: 'Rotherham is not racist. But we want something new to look to'. *The Guardian*. www.theguardian.com/politics/2016/may/22/brexit-britain-rotherham-not-racist

Heritage Lottery Fund (HLF) (2015) https://www.hlf.org.uk/all-our-stories-evaluation

Hewstone, K. and Schmid, M. (2014) Neighbourhood ethnic diversity and orientation toward Muslims in Britain: The role of intergroup contact, *The Political Quarterly*, 85, 3, 320-25.

Hinson, G. (2000) *Fire in my Bones: Transcendence and the Holy Spirit in African American gospel*, Philadelphia, PA: University of Pennsylvania Press.

Hoggett, P. (1997) *Contested Communities: Experiences, struggles, policies*, Bristol: Policy Press.

Holland, J. (2007) Emotions and research, *Social Research Methodology*, 10, 3, 195-209.

Holmes, D. R. and Marcus, G. E. (2008) Collaboration today and the re-imagination of the classic scene of fieldwork encounter, *Collaborative Anthropologies*, 1, 81-101.

hooks. b. (1955) An Aesthetic of Blackness: Strange and Oppositional, *A Journal of Interarts Inquiry*, 1, 65-72.

hooks, b. (1984) 'Black women: Shaping feminist theory', in hooks, b. (1984) *Feminist Theory: From margin to centre*, Boston: South End Press, 1-15.

Hopkins, P. E. (2010) *Young People. Place and Identity*, London: Routledge.

Hoyt, C. L. and Simon, S. (2011) Female leaders: injurious or inspiring role models for women, *Psychology of Women Quarterly*, 35, 1, 143-57.

Hubbard, G., Backett-Milburn, K. and Kemmer, D. (2001) 'Working with emotion: issues for the researcher in fieldwork and teamwork', in Emerald, E. and Carpenter, L. (2015) Vulnerability and Emotions in Research: Risks, Dilemmas and Doubts, *Qualitative Inquiry*, 21 8, 741–750.

Hulteen. B and Wallis, J. (1992) *America's Original Sin: A Study Guide to White Racism*, Washington D.C.: Sojournes.

Hyatt, S. B. (2013) *The Neighborhood of Saturdays: Memories of a multi-ethnic community on Indianapolis' South Side*, Indianapolis: Dog Ear Publishing.

Hyatt, S. (2014) 'Making history through community action', Paper given at the 'Imagine' 2nd Annual Conference, Huddersfield, September 2014.

Hymes, D. (ed) (1972) *Reinventing Anthropology*, New York: Pantheon.

Ingold, T. (2013) *Making. Anthropology, archaeology, art and architecture*, London: Routledge.

Ingold, T. (2014) That's enough about ethnography, *Hau: Journal of Ethnographic Theory*, 4, 1, 383-95.

Jackson, S. (2010) Learning through social spaces: migrant women and lifelong learning in post-colonial London, *International Journal of Lifelong Education*, 29, 2, 237-53.

Jacobson, J. (1997) Religion and ethnicity: dual and alternative sources of identity among Young British Pakistanis, *Ethnic and Racial Studies*, 20, 2, 238-56.

Jay, A. (2014) *Independent Inquiry into Child Sexual Exploitation in Rotherham (1997–2013)*, www.rotherham.gov.uk/downloads/file/1407/independent_inquiry_cse_in_rotherham

Johnson, W. D. (2016) *Antebellum American Women's Poetry: A rhetoric of sentiment*, Southern Illinois University Press.

Jones, M. (1995) *Aspects of Rotherham Volume 1: Discovering Local History*, Barnsley: Wharncliffe.

Jones, M. (1996) *Aspects of Rotherham Volume 2: Discovering Local History*, Barnsley: Wharncliffe.

Jones, M. (2002) *Aspects of Rotherham Volume 3: Discovering Local History*, Barnsley: Wharncliffe.

Kaur, R. and Kalra, V. S. (1996) 'New paths for South Asian identity and musical creativity', in Sharma, A., Hutnyk, J., Sharma, S. (eds) *Dis-orienting Rhythms: The politics of the new Asian dance music*, London: Zed Books, 217-31.

Kay, J. (1991) *The Adoption Papers*, Northumberland: Bloodaxe Books Ltd.

Kay, J. (1997) *Off Colour*, Northumberland: Bloodaxe Books Ltd.

Kay, J. (2011) *Red Dust Road*, London: Picador.

Kester, G. H. (2004) *Conversation Pieces: Community and communication in modern art*, Durham, NC: Duke University Press.

Killingray, D. (2011) Immigrant communities and British local history, *The Local Historian*, 41, 1, 4-12.

Kimbell, L. and Macdonald, H. (2015) *Applying Design Approaches to Policy Making: Discovering Policy Lab*, University of Brighton.

Kress, G. (2010) *Multimodality: A social semiotic approach to contemporary communication*, London: Routledge.

Kuokkanen, R. (2008) *Reshaping the University: Responsibility, indigenous epistemes, and the logic of the gift*, Vancouver: UBC Press.

Lacy, T. (2014) *Thinking Like a Gramscian Historian: An introduction, a provocation, and guide to the basics*, https://s-usih.org/2014/02/thinking-like-a-gramscian-historian/

Ladson-Billings G. and Tate, W. E. (1995) Towards a critical race theory of education, *Teachers' College Record*, 97, 1, 47-68.

Ladson-Billings, G. and Gillborn, D. (eds) (2014) *The RouledgeFalmer Reader In Multicultural Education*, London: RoutledgeFalmer.

Lassiter, L.E. (1998) *The Power of Kiowa Song: A collaborative ethnography*, Tucson: University of Arizona Press.

Lassiter, L.E. (2005) *The Chicago guide to collaborative ethnography*, Chicago: University of Chicago Press.

Lassiter, L.E. (2008) 'Editor's introduction', in Lassiter, L.E. (ed.) *Collaborative Anthropologies*, 1, Lincoln: University of Nebraska Press, vii-xii.

Lassiter, L.E. (forthcoming a) 'Collaborative ethnography: trends, developments, and opportunities', in Shawan, S. E., Branco, C. and Diamond, B. (eds) *Transforming Ethnomusicology*, Oxford: Oxford University Press.

Lassiter, L.E. (forthcoming b) 'Collaborative ethnography: what is it and how can you start doing it?', in Hamilton, L. and Ravenscroft, J. (eds) *Building Research Design in Education: Theoretically informed advanced methods*, London: Bloomsbury.

Lassiter, L. E. and Campbell, E. (2010) What will we have ethnography do?, *Qualitative Inquiry*, 16, 9, 757-67.

Lassiter, L. E. and Campbell, E. (2014) 'Engagement: Participant observation and observant participant', in Lassiter, L. E. and Campbell, B. (2014) *Doing Ethnography Today: Theories, methods, exercises*, Wiley-Blackwell.

Lassiter, L. E., Ellis, C. and Kotay, R. (2002) *The Jesus Road: Kiowas, Christianity, and Indian hymns*, Lincoln, NE: University of Nebraska Press.

Lassiter, L. E., Goodall, H., Campbell, E. and Johnson, M. N. (eds) (2004) *The Other Side of Middletown: Exploring Muncie's African American community*, Walnut Creek: Altamira Press.

Lawless, E. J. (1992) "I was afraid someone like you... an outsider... would misunderstand": Negotiating interpretive differences between ethnographers and subjects, *The Journal of American Folklore*, 105, 417, 302-14.

Lawless, E. J. (2000) "Reciprocal" ethnography: No one said it was easy, *Journal of Folklore Research*, 37, 2/3, 197-205.

Leah, R. (1995) Aboriginal women and everyday racism in Alberta: From lived experience of racism to strategies for personal healing and collective resistance, *The Journal of Human Justice*, 16, 2, 10-29.

Leavy, P. (2015) *Method Meets Arts: Arts based research* (2nd edn), New York City: The Guilford Press.

Library of Birmingham (2014) Connecting Histories.

Lloyd, C. (1991) The methodologies of social history: A critical survey and defence of structurism, *History and Theory*, 30, 2, 180-219.

Lloyd, S. and Moore, J. (2015) "Sedimented Histories": Connections, collaborations and co-production in regional history, *History Workshop Journal*, 80, 1, 234-48.

Lockley, A. and Ismail, I. M. (2016) *Policing Protests in Rotherham: Towards a new approach. South Yorkshire Police Crime Commissioner.* www.southyorkshire-pcc.gov.uk/Document-Library/Publications/Review-of-Police-Community-Relations.pdf

Lorde, A. and Clark, C. (2007) *Sister Outsider: Essays and speeches*, Berkeley: Ten Speed Press.

Lynch, J.P and Simon, R.J. (2003) *Immigration the World Over: Statutes, Policies and Practices*, Lanham MD: Rowman and Littlefield.

Magnusson, S. G. (2003) "The singularization of history": Social history and microhistory within the postmodern state of knowledge, *Journal of Social History*, 36, 3, 701-35.

Mah, A. (2012) *Industrial Ruination, Community, and Place: Landscapes and Legacies of Urban Decline*, Toronto: University of Toronto Press.

Mahuika, R. (2008) Kaupapa Māori theory is critical and anti-colonial, *MAI Review*, 3, 4, 1-16.

Marcus, G. E. and Fischer, M. J. (1986) *Anthropology as Cultural Critique: An experimental moment in the human sciences*, Chicago: University of Chicago Press.

Massey, D. (2005) *For Space*, London: Sage Publications.

Mathie, A. and Cunningham, G. (2003) From client to citizens: Assets based community development as a strategy for community development-driven development, *Development in Practice*, 13, 3, 1-13.

McKenzie, L. (2015) *Getting By: Estates, class and culture in austerity Britain*, Bristol: Policy Press.

McKinlay, P. (2006) The challenge of democratic participation in the community development process, *Community Development Journal*, 41, 4, 492-505.

McLaughlin, C. (2003) The Feeling of Finding Out: The Role of Emotions in Research Education, *Action Research*, 11, 1, 65- 78.

McLoughlin, S. (2014) 'Writing Bradistan across the domains of social reality', in Mcloughlin, G., Kabir, J. and Tomalin, E. (eds) *Writing the City in British Asian Diasporas*, London: Routledge, 21-48.

Miah, S. (2012) School desegregation and the politics of 'forced integration', *Race and Class*, 54, 3, 26-38.

Miah, S. (2015) The groomers and the question of race, *Identity papers: A Journal of British and Irish Studies*, 1, 1, 54-66.

Mills, J. (2004) 'Mothers and mother tongue: Perspectives on self-construction by mothers of Pakistani heritage', in Pavlenko, A. and Blackledge, A (eds) *The Negotiation of Identity in Multilingual Contexts*, Clevedon: Multilingual Matters, 161–191.

Moje, E. R. Ciechanowski, K.M., Kramer, K., Ellis, L., Carrillo, R., Collazo, T. (2004) Working towards third space in content area literacy: An example of everyday funds of knowledge and discourse, *Reading Research Quarterly*, 39, 1, 38-70.

Motapanyane, M. (2013) 'Nostalgia and poetry: Reflective on research, creative expression and fieldwork across borders', *Atlantis*, 36, 1, 12-21.

Munford, A. (2003) *Iron & Steel Town: An industrial history of Rotherham*, Stroud: Sutton.

Munslow, A. (1997) *Deconstructing History*, London: Routledge.

Oakley, A. (1981) 'Interviewing women: A contradiction in terms', in Roberts, H. (ed.) *Doing Feminist Research*, London: Routledge and Kegan Paul, 30-61.

Oakley, A. (2005) *The Ann Oakley Reader: Gender, women, social science*, Bristol: Policy Press.

Oakley, A. (2017) The forgotten example of "settlement sociology": Gender, research, communities, universities, and policymaking in Britain and the USA, 1880-1920, *Research for All*, 1, 1, 20-34. DOI 10.18546/RFA.01.1.03.

Organon (n.d.) *Gramsci's Organic Intellectuals*. http://fucktheory.tumblr.com/

Pahl, K. (2014) *Materializing Literacies in Communities: The uses of literacy revisited*, London: Bloomsbury.

Pahl, K. and Pollard, A. (2008) 'Bling – the Asians introduced that to the country': gold and its value within a group of families of South Asian origin in Yorkshire, *Visual Communication*, 7, 2, 170-182.

Pahl, K. and Pollard, A. (2010) The case of the disappearing object: Narratives and artefacts in homes and a museum exhibition from Pakistani heritage families in South Yorkshire, *Museum and Society*, 8, 1, 1-17.

Pahl, K. and Pool, S. (2011) 'Living your life because it's the only life you've got': Participatory research as a site for discovery in a creative project in a primary school in Thurnscoe UK, *Qualitative Research Journal*, 2, 11, 2, 17-37.

Pahl, K. and Rowsell, J. (2010) *Artifactual Literacies: Every object tells a story*, New York: Teachers College Press.

Pahl, K. and Rowsell, J. (2012) *Literacy and Education: The new literacy studies in the classroom* (2nd edn), London: Sage.

Pahl, K. with Pollard, A. and Rafiq, Z. (2009) Changing identities, changing spaces: The Ferham families exhibition in Rotherham, *Moving Worlds*, 9, 2, 80-103.

Pahl, K., Escott, H., Graham, H., Marwood, K., Pool, S. and Ravetz, A. (in press, 2017) 'What is the role of artists in interdisciplinary collaborative projects with universities and communities?', in Facer, K. and Pahl, K. (eds) *Valuing interdisciplinary collaborative research: Beyond impact*, Bristol: Policy Press.

Pahl, R. E. (1984) *Divisions of Labour*, Oxford: Basil Blackwell.

Palmer, H. (1999) The NI interview: Jean 'Binta' Breeze, *News Internationalist Magazine*, https://newint.org/features/1999/03/05/interview

Parekh, B. (2000) Defining British national identity, *The Political Quarterly*, 71,1, 4-14.

Paton, G. (2010) 'Conservative Party conference: schoolchildren "ignorant of the past", says Gove', http://www.telegraph.co.uk/education/educationnews/8043872/Conservative-Part-Conference-schoolchildren-ignorant-of-the-past-says-Gove.html

Peck, W. C., Flower, L. and Higgins, L. (1994) *Community Literacy*, Berkeley, CA: National Center for the Study of Writing, University of California.

Pente, E., Ward, P., Brown, M. and Singh, H. (2015) The co-production of historical knowledge: Implications for the history of identities, *Identity Papers: A Journal of British and Irish Studies*, 1, 1, 32-53.

Petray, T. L. (2012) A walk in the park: Political emotions and ethnographic vacillation in activist research, *Qualitative Research*, 12, 5, 554-64.

Pink, S. (2009) *Doing Sensory Ethnography*, London: Sage.

Ponds, K.T. (2013) 'The Trauma of Racism: America's Original Sin', in Hulteen. B and Wallis, J. (1992) *America's Original Sin: A Study Guide to White Racism*, Washington D.C.: Sojournes.

Pool, S. and Pahl, K. (2015) 'The work of art in the age of mechanical co-production', in O'Brien, D. and Mathews, P. (eds) *After Urban Regeneration: Communities, policy and place*, Bristol: Policy Press, 79-94.

Prendergast, M., Leggo, C., Sameshima, P. (eds) (2009) *Poetic Inquiry: Vibrant voices in the social sciences*, Rotterdam: Sense Publishers.

Rafiq, Z. (2016) Oral history interview with authors.

Rappaport, J. (2008) Beyond participant observation: Collaborative ethnography as theoretical innovation, *Collaborative Anthropologies*, 1, 1-31.

Rasool, Z. (2016) Oral history interview with authors.

Rautio, P. (2014) Mingling and imitating in producing spaces for knowing and being: Insights from a Finnish study of child–matter intra-action, *Childhood*, 21, 4, 461-74.

Ravetz, J. and Ravetz, A. (2016) Seeing the wood from the trees: Social Science 3.0 and the role of visual thinking, *Innovation: The European Journal of Social Science*, 30, 104-20.

Rawlinson, K. (2013) Another Gove U-turn: Mary Seacole will remain on the curriculum, *The Independent*. www.independent.co.uk/news/uk/politics/another-gove-u-turn-mary-seacole-will-remain-on-the-curriculum-8485472.html

Robinson, D. (2008) 'Community cohesion and the politics of communitarianism', in Flint, J. and Robinson, D. (eds) *Community Cohesion in Crisis?: New dimensions of diversity and difference*, Bristol: Policy Press, 15-34.

Rotherham Metropolitan Borough Council (RMBC) (2015) *Views from Rotherham*, Rotherham: RMBC.

Roulstone, S., Law, J., Rush, R., Clegg, J. and Peters, T. (2011) *Investigating the Role of Language in Children's Early Educational Outcomes*, DfE RR134, Bristol: University of the West of England/ Department for Education.

Said, E. (1979) *Orientalism*, New York: Vintage Books.

Schutte, G. (2011) The laugh of the Medusa heard in South African women's poetry, *Scrutiny 2: Issues in English Studies In South Africa*, 16, 2, 42-55.

Seabrook, J. (1984) *The Idea of Neighbourhood: What local politics should be about*, London: Pluto Press.

Seatter, R. (2008) *On the Beach with Chet Baker*, Bridgend: Seren Books.

Shah, M. (2016) Oral history interview with authors.

Sheeran, G. and Sheeran, Y. (2009) No longer the 1948 show: Local history in the 21st century, *The Local Historian*, 39, 4, 314-23.

Siebers, J. and Fell, E. (2012) *An Exploration of the Relation Between the Concepts of 'Community' and 'Future' in Philosophy*, Swindon: AHRC. www.ahrc.ac.uk/documents/project-reports-and-reviews/ connected-communities/an-exploration-of-the-relation-between-the-concepts-of-community-and-future-in-philosophy/

Simecek, K. (2015) Beyond narrative: Poetry, emotions and the perspectival view, *British Journal of Aesthetics*, 55, 4, 497-513.

Singh-Ghuman, P. A. (2010) Have they passed the cricket test? A 'qualitative' study of Asian adolescents, *Journal of Multilingual and Multicultural Development*, 12, 5, 327-46.

Skidmore, P., Bound. K., Hannah Lownsbrough, H. and Bound, K. (2006) *Community participation: Who benefits?*, York: Joseph Rowntree Foundation.

Smyth, J. (2001) Effect of writing about traumatic experiences: The necessity for narrative structure, *Journal of Social Clinical Psychology*, 20, 2, 161-72.

Snell, J. (2013) Dialect, interaction and class positioning at school: From deficit to difference to repertoire, *Language and Education*, 27, 2, 110-28.

Somerville, P. (2016) *Understanding Community: Politics, policy and practice* (2nd edn), Bristol: Policy Press.

Spivak, G. C. (1988) *Can the Subaltern Speak?*, Basingstoke: Macmillan.

Stadlen, N. (2005) *What Mothers Do: Especially when it looks like nothing*, London: Piatkus.

Stean, J. (2006) *Gender and international relations: Issues, Debates and Future Directions*, Cambridge: Polity Press

Stodulka, T. (2014) Emotion work, ethnography, and survival strategies on the streets of Yogyakarta, *Medical Anthropology*, 34, 1, 83-97.

Street, B.V. (2005) 'Understanding and defining literacy', Background Paper Prepared for Education For All Global Marketing Report 2006 *Literacy for Life*, United Nations Educational Scientific and Cultural Organisation, 1-24.

Tarlo, E. (2003) *Unsettling Memories: Narratives of the Emergency in Delhi*, Berkeley: University of California Press.

Tedlock, D. and Mannheim, B. (1995) *The Dialogic Emergence of Culture*, Urbana: University of Illinois Press.

Torri, M. C. (2012) Community gender entrepreneurship and self-help groups: A way forward to foster social capital and truly effective forms of participation among rural poor women?, *Community Development Journal*, 47, 1, 58-76.

Tuan, Y. F. (2001) *Space and Place: The perspective of experience*, Minnesota: University of Minnesota Press.

Tuhiwai Smith, L. T. (1999) *Decolonizing methodologies: Research and indigenous peoples*, London: Zed Books.

United Nations Educational, Scientific and Cultural Organization (UNESCO) (2003) *Education in a Multicultural World*, UNESCO Education Position Paper, 8-38.

Vasili, P. (1998) *The First Black Footballer: Arthur Wharton 1865-1930: An absence of memory*, London: Frank Cass.

Vergunst, J. (2010) Rhythms of walking: History and presence in a city street, *Space and Culture*, 13, 4, 376-88.

Virsa (n.d.), www.virsa.info

Visram, R. (2002) *Asians in Britain: 400 years of history* (2nd edn), London: Pluto.

Ward, P. (2004) *Britishness since 1870*, Routledge.

Ward, P. and Pente, E. (forthcoming 2017) 'Let's change history! Community histories and the co-production of historical knowledge', in Fraser, L., Hill, M., Murray, S., Pickles, K. and Ryan G. (eds) *History Making a Difference: New approaches*, Cambridge Scholars Press.

Whitmarsh, J. (2011) Out of the mouth of babes: First-time disadvantaged mothers and their perceptions of infant communication, *International Journal of Early Years Education*, 19, 3-4, 283-96.

Williams, R. (1985) *Towards 2000*, London: Pelican.

Williams, R. (1989 [1958]) *Resources of Hope: Culture, democracy, Socialism*, London: Verso.

Willmott, P. and Young, M. (1957) *Family and Kinship in East London*, London: Penguin.

Wills, J. (2016) *Locating Localism: Statecraft, citizenship and democracy*, Bristol: Policy Press.

Yakoubian, B. R. and Yakoubian, J. R. (2017) *Research Processes and Indigenous Communities in Western Alaska: Workshop report*, Kawerak, Inc. www.kawerak.org/forms/nr/Research%20Processes%20and%20 Indigenous%20Communities%20in%20Western%20Alaska%20 Workshop%20Report.pdf

Zalipour, A. (2011) From poetic imagination to imagining: Contemporary notions of poetic imagination in poetry, *Repkatha Journal of Interdisciplinary Studies in Humanities*, 3, 4, 481–94.

Zamindar, V. (2007) *The Long Partition and the Making of Modern South Asia: Refugees, boundaries, histories*, New York: Columbia University Press.

Index